March ✓ W9-AYV-017

Mark,

Perhaps some day you will be
Dean of St. Paul's. Don't preach
these sermons there; the congregation
has heard them before!
With congratulations, love, and prayers,
Nancy Webb
St. Paul's, Charlottesville

JOHN DONNE
DEVOTIONS
UPON EMERGENT OCCASIONS

Together with
DEATH'S DUEL

ANN ARBOR PAPERBACKS
The University of Michigan Press

Fifth printing 1975
First edition as an Ann Arbor Paperback 1959
All rights reserved
ISBN 0-472-06030-9
Published in the United States of America by
The University of Michigan Press and simultaneously
in Don Mills, Canada, by Longman Canada Limited
Manufactured in the United States of America

CONTENTS

THE

LIFE OF DR. JOHN DONNE

(Taken from the life by Izaak Walton).

MASTER JOHN DONNE was born in London, in the year 1573, of good and virtuous parents: and, though his own learning and other multiplied merits may justly appear sufficient to dignify both himself and his posterity, yet the reader may be pleased to know that his father was masculinely and lineally descended from a very ancient family in Wales, where many of his name now live, that deserve and have great reputation in that country.

By his mother he was descended of the family of the famous and learned Sir Thomas More, sometime Lord Chancellor of England: as also, from that worthy and laborious Judge Rastall, who left posterity the vast Statutes of the Law of this nation most exactly abridged.

He had his first breeding in his father's house, where a private tutor had the care of him, until the tenth year of his age; and, in his eleventh year, was sent to the University of Oxford, having at that time a good command both of the French and Latin tongue. This, and some other of his remarkable abilities, made one then give this censure of him: That this age had brought forth another Picus Mirandula; of whom story says, that he was rather born than made wise by study.

There he remained for some years in Hart Hall, having, for the advancement of his studies, tutors of several sciences to attend and instruct him, till time made him capable, and his learning expressed in public exercises, declared him worthy, to receive his first degree in the schools, which he forbore by advice from his friends, who, being for their religion of the Romish persuasion, were conscionably averse to some parts of the oath that is always tendered at those times, and not to be refused by those that expect the titulary honour of their studies.

About the fourteenth year of his age he was transplanted from Oxford to Cambridge, where, that he might receive nourishment from both soils, he staid till his seventeenth year; all which time he was a most laborious student, often changing his studies, but endeavouring to take no degree, for the reasons formerly mentioned.

About the seventeenth year of his age he was removed to London, and then admitted into Lincoln's Inn, with an intent to study the law, where he gave great testimonies of his wit, his learning, and of his improvement in that profession; which never served him for other use than an ornament and self-satisfaction.

His father died before his admission into this society; and, being a merchant, left him his portion in money. (It was £3,000.) His mother, and those to whose care he was committed, were watchful to improve his knowledge, and to that end appointed him tutors both in the mathematics, and in all the other liberal sciences, to attend him. But, with these arts, they were advised to instil into him particular principles of the

Romish Church; of which those tutors professed, though secretly, themselves to be members.

They had almost obliged him to their faith; having for their advantage, besides many opportunities, the example of his dear and pious parents, which was a most powerful persuasion, and did work much upon him, as he professeth in his preface to his " Pseudo-Martyr," a book of which the reader shall have some account in what follows.

He was now entered into the eighteenth year of his age; and at that time had betrothed himself to no religion that might give him any other denomination than a Christian. And reason and piety had both persuaded him that there could be no such sin as schism, if an adherence to some visible Church were not necessary.

About the nineteenth year of his age, he, being then unresolved what religion to adhere to, and considering how much it concerned his soul to choose the most orthodox, did therefore,—though his youth and health promised him a long life—to rectify all scruples that might concern that, presently lay aside all study of the law, and of all other sciences that might give him a denomination; and began seriously to survey and consider the body of Divinity, as it was then controverted betwixt the Reformed and the Roman Church. And, as God's blessed Spirit did then awaken him to the search, and in that industry did never forsake him—they be his own words (in his preface to " Pseudo-Martyr ")—so he calls the same Holy Spirit to witness this protestation; that in that disquisition and search he proceeded with humility and diffidence in himself; and by that which he took to be the safest way; namely, frequent prayers, and an indifferent affection to both parties; and, indeed, Truth had too much light about her to be hid from so sharp an inquirer; and he had too much ingenuity not to acknowledge he had found her.

Being to undertake this search, he believed the Cardinal Bellarmine to be the best defender of the Roman cause, and therefore betook himself to the examination of his reasons. The cause was weighty, and wilful delays had been inexcusable both towards God and his own conscience: he therefore proceeded in this search with all moderate haste, and about the twentieth year of his age did show the then Dean of Gloucester—whose name my memory hath now lost—all the Cardinal's works marked with many weighty observations under his own hand; which works were bequeathed by him, at his death, as a legacy to a most dear friend.

About a year following he resolved to travel: and the Earl of Essex going first to Cales, and after the Island voyages, the first anno 1596, the second 1597, he took the advantage of those opportunities, waited upon his Lordship, and was an eye-witness of those happy and unhappy employments.

But he returned not back into England till he had staid some years, first in Italy and then in Spain, where he made many useful observations of those countries, their laws and manner of government, and returned perfect in their languages.

The time that he spent in Spain was, at his first going into Italy, designed for travelling to the Holy Land, and for viewing Jerusalem and the Sepulchre of our Saviour. But at his being in the furthest parts of Italy, the disappointment of company, or of a safe convoy, or the uncertainty of returns of money into those remote parts, denied him that happiness, which he did often occasionally mention with a deploration.

Not long after his return into England, that exemplary pattern of gravity and wisdom, the Lord Ellesmere, then Keeper of the Great Seal, the Lord Chancellor of England, taking notice of his learning, languages, and other abilities, and much affecting his person and behaviour, took him to be his chief secretary; supposing and intending it to be an introduction to some more weighty employment in the State; for which, his Lordship did often protest, he thought him very fit.

Nor did his Lordship, in this time of Master Donne's attendance upon him, account him to be so much his servant as to forget he was his friend; and, to testify it, did always use him with much courtesy, appointing him a place at his own table, to which he esteemed his company and discourse to be a great ornament.

He continued that employment for the space of five years, being daily useful, and not mercenary to his friend. During which time he—I dare not say unhappily—fell into such a liking, as,—with her approbation,—increased into a love, with a young gentlewoman that lived in that family, who was niece to the Lady Ellesmere, and daughter to Sir George More, then Chancellor of the Garter and Lieutenant of the Tower.

Sir George had some intimation of it, and, knowing prevention to be a great part of wisdom, did therefore remove her with much haste from that to his own house at Lothesley, in the County of Surrey; but too late, by reason of some faithful promises which were so interchangeably passed, as never to be violated by either party.

These promises were only known to themselves;
and the friends of both parties used much diligence,
and many arguments, to kill or cool their affections
to each other; but in vain, for love is a flattering mischief that hath denied aged and wise men a foresight
of those evils that too often prove to be the children
of that blind father; a passion that carries us to commit
errors with as much ease as whirlwinds move feathers,
and begets in us an unwearied industry to the attain-
ment of what we desire.   And such an industry did,
notwithstanding much watchfulness against it, bring
them secretly together,—I forbear to tell the manner
how,—and at last to a marriage too, without the
allowance of those friends whose approbation always
was, and ever will be necessary, to make even a virtuous
love become lawful.

And that the knowledge of their marriage might
not fall, like an unexpected tempest, on those that were
unwilling to have it so; and that pre-apprehensions
might make it the less enormous when it was known,
it was purposely whispered into the ears of many that
it was so, yet by none that could affirm it.   But, to
put a period to the jealousies of Sir George—doubt
often begetting more restless thoughts than the certain
knowledge of what we fear—the news was, in favour
to Mr. Donne, and with his allowance, made known
to Sir George, by his honourable friend and neighbour
Henry, Earl of Northumberland; but it was to Sir
George so immeasurably unwelcome, and so transported him that, as though his passion of anger and
inconsideration might exceed theirs of love and error,
he presently engaged his sister, the Lady Ellesmere, to
join with him to procure her lord to discharge Mr.
Donne of the place he held under his Lordship.   This

request was followed with violence; and though Sir George were remembered that errors might be over punished, and desired therefore to forbear till second considerations might clear some scruples, yet he became restless until his suit was granted and the punishment executed. And though the Lord Chancellor did not, at Mr. Donne's dismission, give him such a commendation as the great Emperor Charles the Fifth did of his Secretary Eraso, when he parted with him to his son and successor, Philip the Second, saying, "That in his Eraso, he gave to him a greater gift than all his estate, and all the kingdoms which he then resigned to him;" yet the Lord Chancellor said, "He parted with a friend, and such a Secretary as was fitter to serve a king than a subject."

Immediately after his dismission from his service, he sent a sad letter to his wife to acquaint her with it; and after the subscription of his name, writ,

" John Donne, Anne Donne, Un-done; "

and God knows it proved too true; for this bitter physic of Mr. Donne's dismission, was not enough to purge out all Sir George's choler, for he was not satisfied till Mr. Donne and his sometime compupil in Cambridge, that married him, namely, Samuel Brooke, who was after Doctor in Divinity and Master of Trinity College—and his brother Mr. Christopher Brooke, sometime Mr. Donne's chamber-fellow in Lincoln's Inn, who gave Mr. Donne his wife, and witnessed the marriage, were all committed to three several prisons.

Mr. Donne was first enlarged, who neither gave rest to his body or brain, nor to any friend in whom

he might hope to have an interest, until he had pro-
cured an enlargement for his two imprisoned friends.

He was now at liberty, but his days were still cloudy;
and, being past these troubles, others did still multiply
upon him; for his wife was—to her extreme sorrow—
detained from him; and though, with Jacob, he endured
not a hard service for her, yet he lost a good one, and
was forced to make good his title, and to get possession
of her by a long and restless suit in law, which proved
troublesome and sadly chargeable to him, whose youth,
and travel, and needless bounty, had brought his estate
into a narrow compass.

It is observed, and most truly, that silence and
submission are charming qualities, and work most
upon passionate men; and it proved so with Sir George;
for these, and a general report of Mr. Donne's merits,
together with his winning behaviour,—which, when
it would entice, had a strange kind of elegant irresistible
art;—these, and time, had so dispassionated Sir George,
that, as the world had approved his daughter's choice,
so he also could not but see a more than ordinary
merit in his new son; and this at last melted him into
so much remorse—for love and anger are so like agues
as to have hot and cold fits; and love in parents, though
it may be quenched, yet is easily rekindled, and expires
not till death denies mankind a natural heat—that
he laboured his son's restoration to his place; using to
that end both his own and his sister's power to her
lord; but with no success; for his answer was, " That
though he was unfeignedly sorry for what he had
done, yet it was inconsistent with his place and credit,
to discharge and readmit servants at the request of
passionate petitioners."

Sir George's endeavour for Mr. Donne's readmission was by all means to be kept secret:—for men do more naturally reluct for errors than submit to put on those blemishes that attend their visible acknowledgment. But, however, it was not long before Sir George appeared to be so far reconciled as to wish their happiness, and not to deny them his paternal blessing, but yet refused to contribute any means that might conduce to their livelihood.

Mr. Donne's estate was the greatest part spent in many and chargeable travels, books, and dear-bought experience: he out of all employment that might yield a support for himself and wife, who had been curiously and plentifully educated; both their natures generous, and accustomed to confer, and not to receive, courtesies; these and other considerations, but chiefly that his wife was to bear a part in his sufferings, surrounded him with many sad thoughts, and some apparent apprehensions of want.

But his sorrows were lessened and his wants prevented by the seasonable courtesy of their noble kinsman, Sir Francis Wolly, of Pirford in Surrey, who intreated them to a cohabitation with him; where they remained with much freedom to themselves, and equal conten to him, for some years; and as their charge increased—she had yearly a child—so did his love and bounty.

Mr. Donne and his wife continued with Sir Francis Wolly till his death: a little before which time Sir Francis was so happy as to make a perfect reconciliation between Sir George and his forsaken son and daughter; Sir George conditioning, by bond, to pay to Mr. Donne 800*l.* at a certain day, as a portion with his wife, or 20*l.* quarterly for their maintenance, as the interest for it, till the said portion was paid.

Most of those years that he lived with Sir Francis he studied the Civil and Canon Laws; in which he acquired such a perfection, as was judged to hold proportion with many, who had made that study the employment of their whole life.

Sir Francis being dead, and that happy family dissolved, Mr. Donne took for himself a house in Mitcham—near to Croydon in Surrey—a place noted for good air and choice company: there his wife and children remained; and for himself he took lodgings in London, near to Whitehall, whither his friends and occasions drew him very often, and where he was as often visited by many of the nobility and others of this nation, who used him in their counsels of greatest consideration, and with some rewards for his better subsistence.

Nor did our own nobility only value and favour him, but his acquaintance and friendship was sought for by most Ambassadors of foreign nations, and by many other strangers whose learning or business occasioned their stay in this nation.

Thus it continued with him for about two years, all which time his family remained constantly at Mitcham; and to which place he often retired himself, and destined some days to a constant study of some points of controversy betwixt the English and Roman Church, and especially those of Supremacy and Allegiance: and to that place and such studies he could willingly have wedded himself during his life; but the earnest persuasion of friends became at last to be so powerful, as to cause the removal of himself and family to London, where Sir Robert Drewry, a gentleman of a very noble estate, and a more liberal mind, assigned him and his wife an useful apartment in his own large house in Drury Lane, and not only rent free, but was also a cherisher of his studies, and such a friend as sympathized with him and his, in all their joy and sorrows.

At this time of Mr. Donne's and his wife's living in Sir Robert's house, the Lord Hay was, by King James, sent upon a glorious embassy to the then French King, Henry the Fourth; and Sir Robert put on a sudden resolution to accompany him to the French Court, and to be present at his audience there. And Sir Robert put on a sudden resolution to solicit Mr. Donne to be his companion in that journey. And this desire was suddenly made known to his wife, who was then with child, and otherwise under so dangerous a habit of body as to her health, that she professed an unwillingness to allow him any absence from her; saying, " Her divining soul boded her some " ill in his absence; " and therefore desired him not to leave her. This made Mr. Donne lay aside all thoughts of the journey, and really to resolve against it. But Sir Robert became restless in his persuasions for it, and Mr. Donne was so generous as to think he had sold his liberty when he received so many charitable kindnesses from him, and told his wife so; who did therefore, with an unwilling willingness, give a faint consent to the journey, which was proposed to be but for two months; for about that time they determined their return. Within a few days after this resolve, the Ambassador, Sir Robert, and Mr. Donne, left London; and were the twelfth day got all safe to Paris. Two days after their arrival there, Mr. Donne was left alone in that room in which Sir Robert, and he, and some other friends had dined together. To this place Sir Robert returned within half an hour; and as he left, so he found, Mr. Donne alone; but in such an ecstasy, and so altered as to his looks, as amazed Sir Robert to behold him; insomuch that he earnestly desired Mr. Donne to declare what had befallen him in the short time of his absence. To which Mr. Donne was not able to make a present answer; but, after a long and perplexed pause, did at last say, " I " have seen a dreadful vision since I saw you: I have " seen my dear wife pass twice by me through this " room, with her hair hanging about her shoulders, " and a dead child in her arms: this I have seen since " I saw you." To which Sir Robert replied, " Sure, " sir, you have slept since I saw you; and this is the " result of some melancholy dream, which I desire " you to forget, for you are now awake." To which Mr. Donne's reply was: " I cannot be surer that I " now live than that I have not slept since I saw you: " and am as sure that at her second appearing she " stopped and looked me in the face, and vanished." Rest and sleep had not altered Mr. Donne's opinion the next day: for he then affirmed this vision with a more deliberate, and so confirmed a confidence, that he inclined Sir Robert to a faint belief that the vision was true. It is truly said that desire and doubt have no rest; and it proved so with Sir Robert; for he immediately sent a servant to Drewry House, with a charge to hasten back and bring him word whether Mrs. Donne were alive; and, if alive, in what condition she was as to her health. The twelfth day the messenger returned with this account:—That he found and left Mrs. Donne very sad and sick in her bed; and that, after a long and dangerous labour, she had been delivered of a dead child. And, upon examination, the abortion proved to be the same day, and about the very hour, that Mr. Donne affirmed he saw her pass by him in his chamber.

This is a relation that will beget some wonder, and it well may; for most of our world are at present possessed with an opinion that visions and miracles are ceased. And, though it is most certain that two lutes, being both strung and tuned to an equal pitch, and then one played upon, the other that is not touched, being laid upon a table at a fit distance, will—like an echo to a trumpet—warble a faint audible harmony in answer to the same tune; yet many will not believe there is any such thing as a sympathy of souls; and I am well pleased that every reader do enjoy his own opinion. But if the unbelieving will not allow the believing reader of this story, a liberty to believe that it may be true, then I wish him to consider many wise men have believed that the ghost of Julius Cæsar did appear to Brutus, and that both St. Austin, and Monica his mother, had visions in order to his conversion. And though these and many others—too many to name—have but the authority of human story, yet the incredible reader may find in the sacred story (1 Sam. xxviii. 14) that Samuel did appear to Saul even after his death—whether really or not, I undertake not to determine. And Bildad, in the Book of Job, says these words (iv. 13–16): " A spirit passed " before my face; the hair of my head stood up; fear " and trembling came upon me, and made all my " bones to shake." Upon which words I will make no comment, but leave them to be considered by the incredulous reader; to whom I will also commend this following consideration: That there be many pious and learned men that believe our merciful God hath assigned to every man a particular guardian angel to be his constant monitor, and to attend him in all his dangers, both of body and soul. And the opinion that every man hath his particular angel may gain some authority by the relation of St. Peter's miraculous deliverance out of prison (Acts xii. 7–10 ; 13–15), not by many, but by one angel. And this belief may yet gain more credit by the reader's considering, that when Peter after his enlargement knocked at the door of Mary the mother of John, and Rhode, the maid-servant, being surprised with joy that Peter was there, did not let him in, but ran in haste and told the disciples, who were then and there met together, that Peter was at the door; and they, not believing it, said she was mad: yet, when she again affirmed it, though they then believed it not, yet they concluded, and said, " It is his angel."

More observations of this nature, and inferences from them, might be made to gain the relation a firmer belief; but I forbear, lest I, that intended to be but a relator, may be thought to be an engaged person for the proving what was related to me; and yet I think myself bound to declare that, though it was not told me by Mr. Donne himself, it was told me—now long since—by a person of honour, and of such intimacy with him, that he knew more of the secrets of his soul than any person then living: and I think he told me the truth; for it was told with such circumstances, and such asseveration, that—to say nothing of my own thoughts—I verily believe he that told it me did himself believe it to be true.

I return from my account of the vision, to tell the reader, that both before Mr. Donne's going into France, at his being there, and after his return, many of the nobility and others that were powerful at court, were watchful and solicitous to the King for some secular employment for him. The King had formerly both known and put a value upon his company, and had also given him some hopes of a state-employment; being always much pleased when Mr. Donne attended him, especially at his meals, where there were usually many deep discourses of general learning, and very often friendly disputes, or debates of religion, betwixt his Majesty and those divines, whose places required their attendance on him at those times: particularly the Dean of the Chapel, who then was Bishop Montague—the publisher of the learned and eloquent Works of his Majesty—and the most Reverend Doctor Andrews the late learned Bishop of Winchester, who was then the King's Almoner.

About this time there grew many disputes, that concerned the Oath of Supremacy and Allegiance, in which the King had appeared, and engaged himself by his public writings now extant: and his Majesty discoursing with Mr. Donne, concerning many of the reasons which are usually urged against the taking of those Oaths, apprehended such a validity and clearness in his stating the questions, and his answers to them, that his Majesty commanded him to bestow some time in drawing the arguments into a method, and then to write his answers to them; and, having done that, not to send, but be his own messenger, and bring them to him. To this he presently and diligently applied himself, and within six weeks brought them to him under his own handwriting, as they be now printed; the book bearing the name of "Pseudo-Martyr," printed anno 1610.

When the King had read and considered that book, he persuaded Mr. Donne to enter into the Ministry;

to which, at that time, he was, and appeared, very unwilling, apprehending it—such was his mistaken modesty—to be too weighty for his abilities.

Such strifes St. Austin had, when St. Ambrose endeavoured his conversion to Christianity; with which he confesseth he acquainted his friend Alipius. Our learned author—a man fit to write after no mean copy—did the like. And declaring his intentions to his dear friend Dr. King, then Bishop of London, a man famous in his generation, and no stranger to Mr. Donne's abilities—for he had been Chaplain to the Lord Chancellor, at the time of Mr. Donne's being his Lordship's Secretary—that reverend man did receive the news with much gladness; and, after some expressions of joy, and a persuasion to be constant in his pious purpose, he proceeded with all convenient speed to ordain him first Deacon, and then Priest not long after.

Presently after he entered into his holy profession, the King sent for him, and made him his Chaplain in Ordinary, and promised to take a particular care for his preferment.

And, though his long familiarity with scholars and persons of greatest quality was such, as might have given some men boldness enough to have preached to any eminent auditory; yet his modesty in this employment was such, that he could not be persuaded to it, but went usually accompanied with some one friend to preach privately in some village, not far from London; his first sermon being preached at Paddington. This he did, till his Majesty sent and appointed him a day to preach to him at Whitehall; and, though much were expected from him, both by his Majesty and others, yet he was so happy—which few are—

as to satisfy and exceed their expectations: preaching the Word so, as shewed his own heart was possessed with those very thoughts and joys that he laboured to distil into others: a preacher in earnest; weeping sometimes for his auditory, sometimes with them; always preaching to himself like an angel from a cloud, but in none; carrying some, as St. Paul was, to Heaven in holy raptures, and enticing others by a sacred art and courtship to amend their lives: here picturing a vice so as to make it ugly to those that practised it; and a virtue so as to make it beloved, even by those that loved it not; and all this with a most particular grace and an unexpressible addition of comeliness.

That summer, in the very same month in which he entered into sacred Orders, and was made the King's Chaplain, his Majesty then going his progress, was entreated to receive an entertainment in the University of Cambridge: and Mr. Donne attending his Majesty at that time, his Majesty was pleased to recommend him to the University, to be made Doctor in Divinity; Doctor Harsnett, after Archbishop of York, was then Vice-Chancellor, who, knowing him to be the author of that learned book the " Pseudo-Martyr," required no other proof of his abilities, but proposed it to the University, who presently assented, and expressed a gladness that they had such an occasion to entitle him to be theirs.

His abilities and industry in his profession were so eminent, and he so known and so beloved by persons of quality, that within the first year of his entering into sacred Orders, he had fourteen advowsons of several benefices presented to him: but they were in the country, and he could not leave his beloved London, to which place he had a natural inclination, having received both his birth and education in it, and there contracted a friendship with many, whose conversation multiplied the joys of his life; but an employment that might affix him to that place would be welcome, for he needed it.

Immediately after his return from Cambridge his wife died, leaving him a man of a narrow, unsettled estate, and—having buried five—the careful father of seven children then living, to whom he gave a voluntary assurance never to bring them under the subjection of a step-mother; which promise he kept most faithfully, burying with his tears all his earthly joys in his most dear and deserving wife's grave, and betook himself to a most retired and solitary life.

In this retiredness, which was often from the sight of his dearest friends, he became crucified to the world, and all those vanities, those imaginary pleasures, that are daily acted on that restless stage, and they were as perfectly crucified to him.

His first motion from his house was to preach where his beloved wife lay buried—in St. Clement's Church, near Temple Bar, London; and his text was a part of the Prophet Jeremy's Lamentation: " Lo, I am the man that have seen affliction."

In this time of sadness he was importuned by the grave Benchers of Lincoln's Inn—who were once the companions and friends of his youth—to accept of their Lecture, which, by reason of Dr. Gataker's removal from thence, was then void; of which he accepted, being most glad to renew his intermitted friendship with those whom he so much loved, and where he had been a Saul,—though not to persecute Christianity, or to deride it, yet in his irregular youth to neglect the visible practice of it,—there to become a Paul, and preach salvation to his beloved brethren.

About which time the Emperor of Germany died, and the Palsgrave, who had lately married the Lady Elizabeth, the King's only daughter, was elected and crowned King of Bohemia, the unhappy beginning of many miseries in that nation.

King James, whose motto—*Beati pacifici*—did truly speak the very thoughts of his heart, endeavoured first to prevent, and after to compose, the discords of that discomposed State; and, amongst other his endeavours, did then send the Lord Hay, Earl of Doncaster, his Ambassador to those unsettled Princes; and, by a special command from his Majesty, Dr. Donne was appointed to assist and attend that employment to the Princes of the Union, for which the Earl was most glad, who had always put a great value on him, and taken a great pleasure in his conversation and discourse: and his friends at Lincoln's Inn were as glad; for they feared that his immoderate study, and sadness for his wife's death, would, as Jacob said, " make his days few," and, respecting his bodily health, "evil" too: and of this there were many visible signs.

About fourteen months after his departure out of England, he returned to his friends of Lincoln's Inn, with his sorrows moderated, and his health improved; and there betook himself to his constant course of preaching.

About a year after his return out of Germany, Dr. Carey was made Bishop of Exeter, and by his removal, the Deanery of St. Paul's being vacant, the King sent to Dr. Donne, and appointed him to attend him at dinner the next day. When his Majesty was sat down, before he had eat any meat, he said after his pleasant manner,

" Dr. Donne, I have invited you to dinner; and, though
" you sit not down with me, yet I will carve to you of a
" dish that I know you love well; for, knowing you
" love London, I do therefore make you Dean of St.
" Paul's; and, when I have dined, then do you take your
" beloved dish home to your study, say grace there to
" yourself, and much good may it do you."

Immediately after he came to his Deanery, he
employed workmen to repair and beautify the Chapel;
suffering as holy David once vowed, " his eyes and temples
" to take no rest till he had first beautified the house of
" God."

The next quarter following when his father-in-law,
Sir George More,—whom time had made a lover and
admirer of him—came to pay to him the conditioned
sum of twenty pounds, he refused to receive it; and said
—as good Jacob did, when he heard his beloved son
Joseph was alive—" ' It is enough; ' you have been kind
" to me and mine: I know your present condition is such
" as not to abound, and I hope mine is, or will be such as
" not to need it: I will therefore receive no more from
" you upon that contract," and in testimony of it freely
gave him up his bond.

Immediately after his admission into his Deanery the
Vicarage of St. Dunstan in the West, London, fell to
him by the death of Dr. White, the advowson of it having
been given to him long before by his honourable friend
Richard Earl of Dorset, then the patron, and confirmed
by his brother the late deceased Edward, both of them
men of much honour.

By these, and another ecclesiastical endowment which
fell to him about the same time, given to him formerly
by the Earl of Kent, he was enabled to become charitable
to the poor, and kind to his friends, and to make such

provision for his children, that they were not left
scandalous as relating to their or his profession and
quality.

The next Parliament, which was within that present
year, he was chosen Prolocutor to the Convocation, and
about that time was appointed by his Majesty, his most
gracious master, to preach very many occasional sermons,
as at St. Paul's Cross, and other places. All which
employments he performed to the admiration of the
representative body of the whole Clergy of this nation.

He was once, and but once, clouded with the King's
displeasure, and it was about this time; which was occasioned by some malicious whisperer, who had told his
Majesty that Dr. Donne had put on the general humour
of the pulpits, and was become busy in insinuating a
fear of the King's inclining to popery, and a dislike of his
government; and particularly for the King's then turning
the evening lectures into catechising, and expounding
the Prayer of our Lord, and of the Belief, and Commandments. His Majesty was the more inclinable to
believe this, for that a person of nobility and great note,
betwixt whom and Dr. Donne there had been a great
friendship, was at this very time discarded the court—
I shall forbear his name, unless I had a fairer occasion—
and justly committed to prison; which begot many
rumours in the common people, who in this nation think
they are not wise unless they be busy about what they
understand not, and especially about religion.

The King received this news with so much discontent
and restlessness that he would not suffer the sun to set
and leave him under this doubt; but sent for Dr. Donne,
and required his answer to the accusation; which was so
clear and satisfactory that the King said, " he was right
" glad he rested no longer under the suspicion." When

the King had said this, Dr. Donne kneeled down, and thanked his Majesty, and protested his answer was faithful, and free from all collusion, and therefore " desired " that he might not rise till, as in like cases, he always " had from God, so he might have from his Majesty, " some assurance that he stood clear and fair in his " opinion." At which the King raised him from his knees with his own hands, and " protested he believed " him; and that he knew he was an honest man, and " doubted not but that he loved him truly." And, having thus dismissed him, he called some Lords of his Council into his chamber, and said with much earnestness, " My Doctor is an honest man; and, my Lords, I was " never better satisfied with an answer than he hath now " made me; and I always rejoice when I think that by " my means he became a Divine."

He was made Dean in the fiftieth year of his age, and in his fifty-fourth year a dangerous sickness seized him, which inclined him to a consumption; but God, as Job thankfully acknowledged, preserved his spirit, and kept his intellectuals as clear and perfect as when that sickness first seized his body; but it continued long, and threatened him with death, which he dreaded not.

Within a few days his distempers abated; and as his strength increased so did his thankfulness to Almighty God, testified in his most excellent " Book of Devotions," which he published at his recovery; in which the reader may see the most secret thoughts that then possessed his soul, paraphrased and made public: a book that may not unfitly be called a Sacred Picture of Spiritual Ecstasies, occasioned and applicable to the emergencies of that sickness; which book, being a composition of meditations, disquisitions, and prayers, he writ on his sick-bed; herein imitating the holy Patriarchs, who were wont to build their altars in that place where they had received their blessings.

This sickness brought him so near to the gates of death, and he saw the grave so ready to devour him, that he would often say his recovery was supernatural: but that God that then restored his health continued it to him till the fifty-ninth year of his life: and then, in August 1630, being with his eldest daughter, Mrs. Harvey, at Abury Hatch, in Essex, he there fell into a fever, which, with the help of his constant infirmity—vapours from the spleen—hastened him into so visible a consumption that his beholders might say, as St. Paul of himself, " He dies daily; " and he might say with Job, " My welfare passeth away as a cloud, the days of my " affliction have taken hold of me, and weary nights are " appointed for me."

Reader, this sickness continued long, not only weakening, but wearying him so much, that my desire is he may now take some rest; and that before I speak of his death thou wilt not think it an impertinent digression to look back with me upon some observations of his life, which, whilst a gentle slumber gives rest to his spirits, may, I hope, not unfitly, exercise thy consideration.

His marriage was the remarkable error of his life; an error which, though he had a wit able and very apt to maintain paradoxes, yet he was very far from justifying it: and though his wife's competent years, and other reasons, might be justly urged to moderate severe censures, yet he would occasionally condemn himself for it: and doubtless it had been attended with an heavy repentance, if God had not blessed them with so mutual and cordial affections, as in the midst of their sufferings made their bread of sorrow taste more pleasantly than the banquets of dull and low-spirited people.

The recreations of his youth were poetry, in which he was so happy as if nature and all her varieties had been made only to exercise his sharp wit and high fancy; and in those pieces which were facetiously composed and carelessly scattered,—most of them being written before the twentieth year of his age—it may appear by his choice metaphors that both nature and all the arts joined to assist him with their utmost skill.

It is a truth, that in his penitential years, viewing some of those pieces that had been loosely—God knows, too loosely—scattered in his youth, he wished they had been abortive, or so short-lived that his own eyes had witnessed their funerals; but, though he was no friend to them, he was not so fallen out with heavenly poetry, as to forsake that; no, not in his declining age; witnessed then by many divine sonnets, and other high, holy, and harmonious composures. Yea, even on his former sick-bed he wrote this heavenly hymn, expressing the great joy that then possessed his soul, in the assurance of God's favour to him when he composed it:—

" AN HYMN

" TO GOD THE FATHER.

" Wilt Thou forgive that sin where I begun,
   " Which was my sin, though it were done before?
" Wilt Thou forgive that sin through which I run,
   " And do run still, though still I do deplore?
" When Thou hast done, Thou hast not done,
               " For I have more.

" Wilt Thou forgive that sin, which I have won
   " Others to sin, and made my sin their door?
" Wilt Thou forgive that sin which I did shun
   " A year or two:—but wallow'd in a score?
" When Thou hast done, Thou hast not done,
               " For I have more.

" I have a sin of fear, that when I've spun
  " My last thread, I shall perish on the shore;
" But swear by Thyself, that at my death Thy Son
  " Shall shine as He shines now, and heretofore;
" And having done that, Thou hast done,
                 " I fear no more."

I have the rather mentioned this hymn, for that he caused it to be set to a most grave and solemn tune, and to be often sung to the organ by the choiristers of St. Paul's Church, in his own hearing; especially at the Evening Service; and at his return from his customary devotions in that place, did occasionally say to a friend, " the words " of this hymn have restored to me the same thoughts of " joy that possessed my soul in my sickness, when I " composed it. And, O the power of church-music! " that harmony added to this hymn has raised the affections " of my heart, and quickened my graces of zeal and " gratitude; and I observe that I always return from " paying this public duty of prayer and praise to God, " with an unexpressible tranquillity of mind, and a " willingness to leave the world."

After this manner did the disciples of our Saviour, and the best of Christians in those ages of the Church nearest to His time, offer their praises to Almighty God. And the reader of St. Augustine's life may there find, that towards his dissolution he wept abundantly, that the enemies of Christianity had broke in upon them, and profaned and ruined their sanctuaries, and because their public hymns and lauds were lost out of their Churches. And after this manner have many devout souls lifted up their hands and offered acceptable sacrifices unto Almighty God, where Dr. Donne offered his, and now lies buried.

But now [1656], Oh Lord! how is that place become desolate!

Before I proceed further, I think fit to inform the reader, that not long before his death he caused to be drawn a figure of the Body of Christ extended upon an anchor, like those which painters draw, when they would present us with the picture of Christ crucified on the cross: his varying no otherwise than to affix Him not to a cross, but to an anchor—the emblem of Hope;—this he caused to be drawn in little, and then many of those figures thus drawn to be engraven very small in Heliotropium stones, and set in gold; and of these he sent to many of his dearest friends, to be used as seals, or rings, and kept as memorials of him, and of his affection to them.

His dear friends and benefactors, Sir Henry Goodier and Sir Robert Drewry, could not be of that number; nor could the Lady Magdalen Herbert, the mother of George Herbert, for they had put off mortality, and taken possession of the grave before him; but Sir Henry Wotton, and Dr. Hall, the then—late deceased—Bishop of Norwich, were; and so were Dr. Duppa, Bishop of Salisbury, and Dr. Henry King, Bishop of Chichester—lately deceased—men, in whom there was such a commixture of general learning, of natural eloquence, and Christian humility, that they deserve a commemoration by a pen equal to their own, which none have exceeded.

And in this enumeration of his friends, though many must be omitted, yet that man of primitive piety, Mr. George Herbert, may not; I mean that George Herbert, who was the author of " The Temple, or Sacred Poems " and Ejaculations." A book, in which by declaring his own spiritual conflicts, he hath comforted and raised many a dejected and discomposed soul, and charmed them into sweet and quiet thoughts; a book, by the frequent reading whereof, and the assistance of that Spirit that seemed to inspire the author, the reader may attain habits of peace and piety, and all the gifts of the Holy Ghost and Heaven: and may, by still reading, still keep those sacred fires burning upon the altar of so pure a heart, as shall free it from the anxieties of this world, and keep it fixed upon things that are above. Betwixt this George Herbert and Dr. Donne, there was a long and dear friendship, made up by such a sympathy of inclinations that they coveted and joyed to be in each other's company; and this happy friendship was still maintained by many sacred endearments; of which that which followeth may be some testimony.

" TO MR. GEORGE HERBERT;

" SENT HIM WITH ONE OF MY SEALS OF THE ANCHOR AND CHRIST.

 " *A Sheaf of Snakes used* " *heretofore to be my Seal,* " *which is the Crest of our* " *poor family.*"

" Qui prius assuetus serpentum falce tabellas
  " Signare, hæc nostræ symbola parva domus,
" Adscitus domui Domini——

" Adopted in God's family, and so
" My old coat lost, into new Arms I go.
" The Cross, my Seal in Baptism, spread below,
" Does by that form into an Anchor grow.
" Crosses grow Anchors, bear as thou shouldst do
" Thy Cross, and that Cross grows an Anchor too.
" But He that makes our Crosses Anchors thus,
" Is Christ, who there is crucified for us.
" Yet with this I may my first Serpents hold;—
" God gives new blessings, and yet leaves the old--

" The Serpent, may, as wise, my pattern be;
" My poison, as he feeds on dust, that's me.
" And, as he rounds the earth to murder, sure
" He is my death; but on the Cross, my cure,
" Crucify nature then; and then implore
" All grace from Him, crucified there before.
" When all is Cross, and that Cross Anchor grown
" This Seal's a Catechism, not a Seal alone.
" Under that little Seal great gifts I send,
" Both works and pray'rs, pawns and fruits of a friend.
" O! may that Saint that rides on our Great Seal,
" To you that bear his name, large bounty deal.
                                        " JOHN DONNE."

                " IN SACRAM ANCHORAM PISCATORIS

                " GEORGE HERBERT.

" Quod Crux nequibat fixa clavique additi,—
" Tenere Christum scilicet ne ascenderet,
" Tuive Christum—

" Although the Cross could not here Christ detain,
" When nail'd unto't, but He ascends again;
" Nor yet thy eloquence here keep Him still,
" But only whilst thou speak'st—this Anchor will:
" Nor canst thou be content, unless thou to
" This certain Anchor add a Seal; and so
" The water and the earth both unto thee
" Do owe the symbol of their certainty.
" Let the world reel, we and all ours stand sure,
" This holy cable's from all storms secure.
                                    " GEORGE HERBERT."

I return to tell the reader, that, besides these verses to
his dear Mr. Herbert, and that Hymn that I mentioned
to be sung in the choir of St. Paul's Church, he did also
shorten and beguile many sad hours by composing other
sacred ditties; and he writ an Hymn on his death-bed,
which bears this title:—

"AN HYMN TO GOD, MY GOD, IN MY SICKNESS.

"*March* 23, 1630.

" Since I am coming to that holy room,
　" Where, with Thy Choir of Saints, for evermore
" I shall be made Thy music, as I come
　" I tune my instrument here at the door,
　" And, what I must do then, think here before.

" Since my Physicians by their loves are grown
　" Cosmographers; and I their map, who lie
" Flat on this bed——

" So, in His purple wrapt, receive my Lord!
　" By these His thorns, give me His other Crown
" And, as to other souls I preach'd Thy word,
　" Be this my text, my sermon to mine own,
　" ' That He may raise; therefore the Lord throws down.' "

If these fall under the censure of a soul, whose too much mixture with earth makes it unfit to judge of these high raptures and illuminations, let him know, that many holy and devout men have thought the soul of Prudentius to be most refined, when, not many days before his death, " he charged it to present his God each morning " and evening with a new and spiritual song; " justified by the example of King David and the good King Hezekiah, who, upon the renovation of his years paid his thankful vows to Almighty God in a royal hymn, which he concludes in these words: " The Lord was ready to " save; therefore I will sing my songs to the stringed " instruments all the days of my life in the Temple of " my God."

The latter part of his life may be said to be a continued study; for as he usually preached once a week, if not oftener, so after his sermon he never gave his eyes rest, till he had chosen out a new text, and that night cast his sermon into a form, and his text into divisions; and the next day betook himself to consult the Fathers, and so commit his meditations to his memory, which was excellent. But upon Saturday he usually gave himself and his mind a rest from the weary burthen of his week's meditations, and usually spent that day in visitation of friends, or some other diversions of his thoughts; and would say, " that he gave both his body and mind that " refreshment, that he might be enabled to do the work " of the day following, not faintly, but with courage and " cheerfulness."

Nor was his age only so industrious, but in the most unsettled days of his youth, his bed was not able to detain him beyond the hour of four in a morning; and it was no common business that drew him out of his chamber till past ten; all which time was employed in study; though he took great liberty after it. And if this seem strange, it may gain a belief by the visible fruits of his labours; some of which remain as testimonies of what is here written: for he left the resultance of 1400 authors, most of them abridged and analysed with his own hand: he left also six score of his sermons, all written with his own hand, also an exact and laborious Treatise concerning self-murder, called Biathanatos; wherein all the laws violated by that act are diligently surveyed, and judiciously censured: a Treatise written in his younger days, which alone might declare him then not only perfect in the Civil and Canon Law, but in many other such studies and arguments, as enter not into the consideration of many that labour to be thought great clerks, and pretend to know all things.

Nor were these only found in his study, but all businesses that passed of any public consequence, either in this or any of our neighbour-nations, he abbreviated either in Latin, or in the language of that nation, and kept them by him for useful memorials. So he did the copies of divers Letters and Cases of Conscience that had concerned his friends, with his observations and solutions of them; and divers other businesses of importance, all particularly and methodically digested by himself.

He did prepare to leave the world before life left him; making his Will when no faculty of his soul was damped or made defective by pain or sickness, or he surprised by a sudden apprehension of death: but it was made with mature deliberation, expressing himself an impartial father, by making his children's portions equal; and a lover of his friends, whom he remembered with legacies fitly and discreetly chosen and bequeathed. I cannot forbear a nomination of some of them; for methinks they be persons that seem to challenge a recordation in this place; as namely, to his brother-in-law, Sir Thomas Grimes, he gave that striking clock, which he had long worn in his pocket; to his dear friend and executor, Dr. King—late Bishop of Chichester—that Model of Gold of the Synod of Dort, with which the States presented him at his last being at the Hague; and the two pictures of Padre Paolo and Fulgentio, men of his acquaintance when he travelled Italy, and of great note in that nation for their remarkable learning.—To his ancient friend Dr. Brook—that married him—Master of Trinity College in Cambridge, he gave the picture of the Blessed Virgin and Joseph.—To Dr. Winniff who succeeded him in the Deanery—he gave a picture called the Skeleton.—To the succeeding Dean, who was not then known, he gave many necessaries of worth, and useful for his house; and also several pictures and ornaments for the Chapel, with a desire that they might be registered, and remain as a legacy to his successors.—To the Earls of Dorset and Carlisle he gave several pictures; and so he did to many other friends; legacies, given rather to express his affection, than to make any addition to their estates: but unto the poor he was full of charity, and unto many others, who, by his constant and long continued bounty, might entitle themselves to be his alms-people: for all these he made provision, and so largely, as, having then six children living, might to some appear more than proportionable to his estate. I forbear to mention any more, lest the reader may think I trespass upon his patience: but I will beg his favour, to present him with the beginning and end of his Will.

"In the name of the blessed and glorious Trinity. "Amen. I John Donne, by the mercy of Christ Jesus, "and by the calling of the Church of England, Priest, "being at this time in good health and perfect under- "standing—praised be God therefore—do hereby make "my last Will and Testament in manner and form "following:—

"First, I give my gracious God an entire sacrifice "of body and soul, with my most humble thanks for that "assurance which His Blessed Spirit imprints in me now "of the Salvation of the one, and the Resurrection of the "other; and for that constant and cheerful resolution, "which the same Spirit hath established in me, to live "and die in the religion now professed in the Church of "England. In expectation of that Resurrection, I desire "my body may be buried—in the most private manner "that may be—in that place of St. Paul's Church, "London, that the now Residentiaries have at my request "designed for that purpose, &c.—And this my last Will "and Testament, made in the fear of God,—whose "mercy I humbly beg, and constantly rely upon in Jesus "Christ—and in perfect love and charity with all the "world—whose pardon I ask, from the lowest of my

"servants, to the highest of my superiors—written all
"with my own hand, and my name subscribed to every
"page, of which there are five in number.

"Sealed December 13, 1630."

Nor was this blessed sacrifice of charity expressed only
at his death, but in his life also, by a cheerful and frequent
visitation of any friend whose mind was dejected, or his
fortune necessitous; he was inquisitive after the wants
of prisoners, and redeemed many from prison, that lay
for their fees or small debts: he was a continual giver
to poor scholars, both of this and foreign nations. Besides
what he gave with his own hand, he usually sent a servant,
or a discreet and trusty friend, to distribute his charity to
all the prisons in London, at all the festival times of the
year, especially at the Birth and Resurrection of our
Saviour. He gave an hundred pounds at one time to an
old friend, whom he had known live plentifully, and by
a too liberal heart and carelessness became decayed in
his estate; and when the receiving of it was denied, by
the gentleman's saying, "He wanted not;"—for the
reader may note, that as there be some spirits so generous
as to labour to conceal and endure a sad poverty, rather
than expose themselves to those blushes that attend the
confession of it; so there be others, to whom nature and
grace have afforded such sweet and compassionate souls,
as to pity and prevent the distresses of mankind;—which
I have mentioned because of Dr. Donne's reply, whose
answer was, "I know you want not what will sustain
"nature; for a little will do that; but my desire is, that
"you, who in the days of your plenty have cheered and
"raised the hearts of so many of your dejected friends,
"would now receive this from me, and use it as a cordial
"for the cheering of your own:" and upon these terms
it was received. He was an happy reconciler of many

differences in the families of his friends and kindred,—
which he never undertook faintly; for such undertakings
have usually faint effects—and they had such a faith in
his judgment and impartiality, that he never advised
them to any thing in vain. He was, even to her death,
a most dutiful son to his mother, careful to provide for
her supportation, of which she had been destitute, but
that God raised him up to prevent her necessities; who
having sucked in the religion of the Roman Church
with the mother's milk, spent her estate in foreign
countries, to enjoy a liberty in it, and died in his house
but three months before him.

And to the end it may appear how just a steward
he was of his Lord and Master's revenue, I have thought
fit to let the reader know, that after his entrance into his
Deanery, as he numbered his years, he, at the foot of a
private account, to which God and His Angels were
only witnesses with him,—computed first his revenue,
then what was given to the poor, and other pious uses;
and lastly, what rested for him and his; and having done
that, he then blessed each year's poor remainder with a
thankful prayer; which, for that they discover a more
than common devotion, the reader shall partake some of
them in his own words:—

So all is that remains this year [1624–5]—

" Deo Opt. Max. benigno largitori, á me, at ab iis
" quibus hæc à me reservantur, gloria et gratia in æter-
" num. Amen."

TRANSLATED THUS.

To God all Good, all Great, the benevolent Bestower,
by me and by them, for whom, by me, these sums are laid
up, be glory and grace ascribed for ever. Amen.

So that this year, [1626,] God hath blessed me and mine with—

" Multiplicatæ sunt super nos misericordiæ tuæ,
" Domine."

TRANSLATED THUS.

Thy mercies, Oh Lord! are multiplied upon us.

" Da, Domine, ut quæ ex immensâ bonitate tuâ nobis
" elargiri dignatus sis, in quorumcunque manus de-
" venerint, in tuam semper cedant gloriam. Amen."

TRANSLATED THUS.

Grant, Oh Lord! that what out of Thine infinite bounty Thou hast vouchsafed to lavish upon us, into whosoever hands it may devolve, may always be improved to thy glory. Amen.

" In fine horum sex annorum manet [1627-8-9]—

" Quid habeo quod non accepi a Domino? Largitur
" etiam ut quæ largitus est sua iterum fiant, bono eorum
" usu; ut quemadmodum nec officiis hujus mundi, nec
" loci in quo me posuit dignitati, nec servis, nec egenis,
" in toto hujus anni curriculo mihi conscius sum me
" defuisse; ita et liberi, quibus quæ supersunt, supersunt,
" grato animo ea accipiant, et beneficum authorem
" recognoscant. Amen."

TRANSLATED THUS.

At the end of these six years remains—

What have I, which I have not received from the Lord? He bestows, also, to the intent that what He hath bestowed may revert to Him by the proper use of it: that, as I have not consciously been wanting to myself during the whole course of the past year, either in discharging my secular duties, in retaining the dignity of my station, or in my conduct towards my servants and the poor—so my children for whom remains whatever is remaining, may receive it with gratitude, and acknowledge the beneficent Giver. Amen.

But I return from my long digression.

We left the Author sick in Essex, where he was forced to spend much of that winter, by reason of his disability to remove from that place; and having never, for almost twenty years, omitted his personal attendance on his Majesty in that month, in which he was to attend and preach to him; nor having ever been left out of the roll and number of Lent Preachers, and there being then— in January, 1630—a report brought to London, or raised there, that Dr. Donne was dead; that report gave him occasion to write the following letter to a dear friend:—

" Sir,
" This advantage you and my other friends have by
" my frequent fevers, that I am so much the oftener at
" the gates of Heaven; and this advantage by the solitude
" and close imprisonment that they reduce me to after,
" that I am so much the oftener at my prayers, in which I
" shall never leave out your happiness; and I doubt not,
" among His other blessings, God will add some one to
" you for my prayers. A man would almost be content
" to die—if there were no other benefit in death—to
" hear of so much sorrow, and so much good testimony
" from good men, as I—God be blessed for it—did upon
" the report of my death; yet I perceive it went not
" through all; for one writ to me, that some—and he
" said of my friends—conceived I was not so ill as I
" pretended, but withdrew myself to live at ease, dis-

" charged of preaching. It is an unfriendly, and, God
" knows, an ill-grounded interpretation; for I have
" always been sorrier when I could not preach, than any
" could be they could not hear me. It hath been my
" desire, and God may be pleased to grant it, that I might
" die in the pulpit; if not that, yet that I might take my
" death in the pulpit; that is, die the sooner by occasion
" of those labours. Sir, I hope to see you presently after
" Candlemas; about which time will fall my Lent Sermon
" at Court, except my Lord Chamberlain believe me to
" be dead, and so leave me out of the roll: but as long as I
" live, and am not speechless, I would not willingly,
" decline that service. I have better leisure to write,
" than you to read; yet I would not willingly oppress you
" with too much letter. God so bless you and your son,
" as I wish to

> " Your poor friend and Servant
> " In Christ Jesus,
>
> > " J. DONNE."

Before that month ended, he was appointed to preach
upon his old constant day, the first Friday in Lent: he had
notice of it, and had in his sickness so prepared for that
employment, that as he had long thirsted for it, so he
resolved his weakness should not hinder his journey; he
came therefore to London some few days before his
appointed day of preaching. At his coming thither,
many of his friends—who with sorrow saw his sickness
had left him but so much flesh as did only cover his
bones—doubted his strength to perform that task, and did
therefore dissuade him from undertaking it, assuring him,
however, it was like to shorten his life: but he passionately
denied their requests, saying " he would not doubt that
" that God, who in so many weaknesses had assisted him

" with an unexpected strength, would now withdraw it
" in his last employment; professing an holy ambition to
" perform that sacred work." And when, to the amazement of some beholders, he appeared in the pulpit, many
of them thought he presented himself not to preach
mortification by a living voice, but mortality by a decayed
body, and a dying face. And doubtless many did secretly
ask that question in Ezekiel (chap. xxxvii. 3), " Do
" these bones live? or, can that soul organise that tongue,
" to speak so long time as the sand in that glass will move
" towards its centre, and measure out an hour of this
" dying man's unspent life? Doubtless it cannot." And
yet, after some faint pauses in his zealous prayer, his strong
desires enabled his weak body to discharge his memory of
his preconceived meditations, which were of dying; the
text being, " To God the Lord belong the issues from
" death." Many that then saw his tears, and heard his
faint and hollow voice, professing they thought the text
prophetically chosen, and that Dr. Donne had preached
his own Funeral Sermon.

Being full of joy that God had enabled him to perform
this desired duty, he hastened to his house; out of which
he never moved, till, like St. Stephen, " he was carried
" by devout men to his grave."

The next day after his sermon, his strength being much
wasted, and his spirits so spent as indisposed him to
business or to talk, a friend that had often been a witness
of his free and facetious discourse asked him, " Why are
" you sad? " To whom he replied with a countenance
so full of cheerful gravity, as gave testimony of an inward
tranquillity of mind, and of a soul willing to take a farewell of this world, and said:—

" I am not sad; but most of the night past I have enter-
" tained myself with many thoughts of several friends that

" have left me here, and are gone to that place from which
" they shall not return; and that within a few days I also
" shall go hence, and be no more seen. And my prepara-
" tion for this change is become my nightly meditation
" upon my bed, which my infirmities have now made
" restless to me. But at this present time, I was in a
" serious contemplation of the providence and goodness
" of God to me; to me, who am less than the least of His
" mercies: and looking back upon my life past, I now
" plainly see it was His hand that prevented me from all
" temporal employment; and that it was His will I should
" never settle nor thrive till I entered into the Ministry;
" in which I have now lived almost twenty years—I
" hope to His glory,—and by which, I most humbly
" thank Him, I have been enabled to requite most of those
" friends which shewed me kindness when my fortune
" was very low, as God knows it was: and—as it hath
" occasioned the expression of my gratitude—I thank
" God most of them have stood in need of my requital.
" I have lived to be useful and comfortable to my good
" Father-in-law, Sir George More, whose patience God
" hath been pleased to exercise with many temporal
" crosses; I have maintained my own mother, whom it
" hath pleased God, after a plentiful fortune in her younger
" days, to bring to great decay in her very old age. I
" have quieted the consciences of many, that have groaned
" under the burden of a wounded spirit, whose prayers I
" hope are available for me. I cannot plead innocency
" of life, especially of my youth; but I am to be judged
" by a merciful God, who is not willing to see what I
" have done amiss. And though of myself I have nothing
" to present to Him but sins and misery, yet I know He
" looks not upon me now as I am of myself, but as I am
" in my Saviour, and hath given me, even at this present

" time, some testimonies by His Holy Spirit, that I am of
" the number of His Elect: I am therefore full of inexpres-
" sible joy, and shall die in peace."

I must here look so far back, as to tell the reader that
at his first return out of Essex, to preach his last sermon,
his old friend and physician, Dr. Fox—a man of great
worth—came to him to consult his health; and that after
a sight of him, and some queries concerning his distempers
he told him, " That by cordials, and drinking milk twenty
" days together, there was a probability of his restoration
" to health " ; but he passionately denied to drink it.
Nevertheless, Dr. Fox, who loved him most entirely,
wearied him with solicitations, till he yielded to take it
for ten days; at the end of which time he told Dr. Fox,
" He had drunk it more to satisfy him, than to recover
" his health; and that he would not drink it ten days
" longer, upon the best moral assurance of having twenty
" years added to his life; for he loved it not; and was so
" far from fearing Death, which to others is the King of
" Terrors, that he longed for the day of his dissolution."

It is observed, that a desire of glory or commendation
is rooted in the very nature of man; and that those of the
severest and most mortified lives, though they may become
so humble as to banish self-flattery, and such weeds as
naturally grow there; yet they have not been able to kill
this desire of glory, but that like our radical heat, it will
both live and die with us; and many think it should do so;
and we want not sacred examples to justify the desire of
having our memory to outlive our lives; which I mention,
because Dr. Donne, by the persuasion of Dr. Fox, easily
yielded at this very time to have a monument made for
him; but Dr. Fox undertook not to persuade him how, or
what monument it should be; that was left to Dr. Donne
himself.

A monument being resolved upon, Dr. Donne sent for a carver to make for him in wood the figure of an urn, giving him directions for the compass and height of it; and to bring with it a board, of the just height of his body. " These being got, then without delay a choice painter " was got to be in readiness to draw his picture, which was " taken as followeth.—Several charcoal fires being first " made in his large study, he brought with him into that " place his winding-sheet in his hand, and having put off " all his clothes, had this sheet put on him, and so tied with " knots at his head and feet, and his hands so placed as " dead bodies are usually fitted, to be shrouded and put " into their coffin, or grave. Upon this urn he thus " stood, with his eyes shut, and with so much of the sheet " turned aside as might shew his lean, pale, and death-like " face, which was purposely turned towards the East, " from whence he expected the second coming of his and " our Saviour Jesus." In this posture he was drawn at his just height; and when the picture was fully finished, he caused it to be set by his bedside, where it continued and became his hourly object till his death, and was then given to his dearest friend and executor Dr. Henry King, then chief Residentiary of St. Paul's, who caused him to be thus carved in one entire piece of white marble, as it now stands in that Church; and by Dr. Donne's own appointment, these words were to be affixed to it as an epitaph:—

JOHANNES DONNE

SAC. THEOL. PROFESS.
POST VARIA STUDIA, QUIBUS AB ANNIS
TENERRIMIS FIDELITER, NEC INFELICITER
INCUBUIT;
INSTINCTU ET IMPULSU SP. SANCTI, MONITU
ET HORTATU
REGIS JACOBI, ORDINES SACROS AMPLEXUS,
ANNO SUI JESU, MDCXIV. ET SUÆ ÆTATIS XLII.
DECANATU HUJUS ECCLESIÆ INDUTUS,
XXVII. NOVEMBRIS, MDCXXI.
EXUTUS MORTE ULTIMO DIE MARTII, MDCXXXI.
HIC LICET IN OCCIDUO CINERE, ASPICIT EUM
CUJUS NOMEN EST ORIENS.

And now, having brought him through the many labyrinths and perplexities of a various life, even to the gates of death and the grave; my desire is, he may rest, till I have told my reader that I have seen many pictures of him, in several habits, and at several ages, and in several postures: and I now mention this because I have seen one picture of him, drawn by a curious hand, at his age of eighteen, with his sword, and what other adornments might then suit with the present fashions of youth and the giddy gaieties of that age; and his motto then was—

" How much shall I be changed
" Before I am changed! "

And if that young, and his now dying picture were at this time set together, every beholder might say, " Lord! how much is Dr. Donne already changed, before he is changed! " And the view of them might give my reader occasion to ask himself with some amazement, " Lord! how much may I also, that am " now in health, be changed before I am changed;

xlvi

" before this vile, this changeable body shall put off
" mortality! " and therefore to prepare for it.—But this
is not writ so much for my reader's memento, as to tell
him, that Dr. Donne would often in his private discourses,
and often publicly in his sermons, mention the many
changes both of his body and mind, especially of his mind
from a vertiginous giddiness; and would as often say,
" His great and most blessed change was from a temporal
" to a spiritual employment "; in which he was so happy,
that he accounted the former part of his life to be lost;
and the beginning of it to be, from his first entering into
Sacred Orders, and serving his most merciful God at
His altar.

Upon Monday, after the drawing this picture, he took
his last leave of his beloved study; and, being sensible of
his hourly decay, retired himself to his bed-chamber; and
that week sent at several times for many of his most con-
siderable friends, with whom he took a solemn and
deliberate farewell, commending to their considerations
some sentences useful for the regulation of their lives;
and then dismissed them, as good Jacob did his sons, with
a spiritual benediction. The Sunday following, he
appointed his servants, that if there were any business yet
undone, that concerned him or themselves, it should be
prepared against Saturday next; for after that day he
would not mix his thoughts with any thing that concerned
this world; nor ever did; but, as Job, so he " waited for
" the appointed day of his dissolution."

And now he was so happy as to have nothing to do but
to die, to do which he stood in need of no longer time; for
he had studied it long, and to so happy a perfection, that
in a former sickness he called God to witness (in his
" Book of Devotions," written then), " He was that
" minute ready to deliver his soul into his Hands, if that

" minute God would determine his dissolution." In that sickness he begged of God the constancy to be preserved in that estate for ever; and his patient expectation to have his immortal soul disrobed from her garment of mortality, makes me confident that he now had a modest assurance that his prayers were then heard, and his petition granted. He lay fifteen days earnestly expecting his hourly change; and in the last hour of his last day, as his body melted away, and vapoured into spirit, his soul having, I verily believe, some revelation of the beatifical vision, he said, " I were miserable if I might not die "; and after those words, closed many periods of his faint breath by saying often, " Thy kingdom come, Thy will " be done." His speech, which had long been his ready and faithful servant, left him not till the last minute of his life, and then forsook him, not to serve another master —for who speaks like him,—but died before him; for that it was then become useless to him, that now conversed with God on earth as Angels are said to do in heaven, only by thoughts and looks. Being speechless, and seeing heaven by that illumination by which he saw it, he did, as St. Stephen ," look stedfastly into it, till he saw the Son of " Man standing at the right hand of God His Father "; and being satisfied with this blessed sight, as his soul ascended, and his last breath departed from him, he closed his own eyes, and then disposed his hands and body into such a posture, as required not the least alteration by those that came to shroud him.

Thus variable, thus virtuous was the life; thus excellent, thus exemplary was the death of this memorable man.

He was buried in that place of St. Paul's Church, which he had appointed for that use some years before his death; and by which he passed daily to pay his public devotions to Almighty God—who was then served twice a day by a public form of prayer and praises in that place; but he was not buried privately, though he desired it; for, beside an unnumbered number of others, many persons of nobility, and of eminence for learning, who did love and honour him in his life, did show it at his death, by a voluntary and sad attendance of his body to the grave, where nothing was so remarkable as a public sorrow.

To which place of his burial some mournful friends repaired, and, as Alexander the Great did to the grave of the famous Achilles, so they strewed his with an abundance of curious and costly flowers; which course they—who were never yet known—continued morning and evening for many days, not ceasing till the stones that were taken up in that Church to give his body admission into the cold earth—now his bed of rest—were again by the mason's art so levelled and firmed as they had been formerly, and his place of burial undistinguishable to common view.

The next day after his burial some unknown friend, some one of the many lovers and admirers of his virtue and learning, writ this epitaph with a coal on the wall over his grave:—

" Reader! I am to let thee know,
" Donne's body only lies below;
" For, could the grave his soul comprise,
" Earth would be richer than the skies! "

Nor was this all the honour done to his reverend ashes; for, as there be some persons that will not receive a reward for that for which God accounts Himself a debtor; persons that dare trust God with their charity, and without a witness; so there was by some grateful unknown friend, that thought Dr. Donne's memory ought to be perpetuated, an hundred marks sent to his faithful friends and executors (Dr. King and Dr. Montford), towards the making of his monument. It was not for many years known by whom; but, after the death of Dr. Fox, it was known that it was he that sent it; and he lived to see as lively a representation of his dead friend as marble can express: a statue indeed so like Dr. Donne, that—as his friend Sir Henry Wotton hath expressed himself—" It " seems to breathe faintly, and posterity shall look upon " it as a kind of artificial miracle."

He was of stature moderately tall; of a straight and equally-proportioned body, to which all his words and actions gave an unexpressible addition of comeliness.

The melancholy and pleasant humour were in him so contempered, that each gave advantage to the other, and made his company one of the delights of mankind.

His fancy was unimitably high, equalled only by his great wit; both being made useful by a commanding judgment.

His aspect was cheerful, and such as gave a silent testimony of a clear knowing soul, and of a conscience at peace with itself.

His melting eye showed that he had a soft heart, full of noble compassion; of too brave a soul to offer injuries, and too much a Christian not to pardon them in others.

He did much contemplate—especially after he entered into his sacred calling—the mercies of Almighty God, the immortality of the soul, and the joys of heaven: and would often say in a kind of sacred ecstacy—" Blessed be " God that He is God, only and divinely like Himself."

He was by nature highly passionate, but more apt to reluct at the excesses of it. A great lover of the offices of humanity, and of so merciful a spirit that he never beheld the miseries of mankind without pity and relief.

He was earnest and unwearied in the search of know-

1

ledge, with which his vigorous soul is now satisfied, and employed in a continual praise of that God that first breathed it into his active body: that body which once was a temple of the Holy Ghost, and is now become a small quantity of Christian dust:—

But I shall see it re-animated.

I.W.

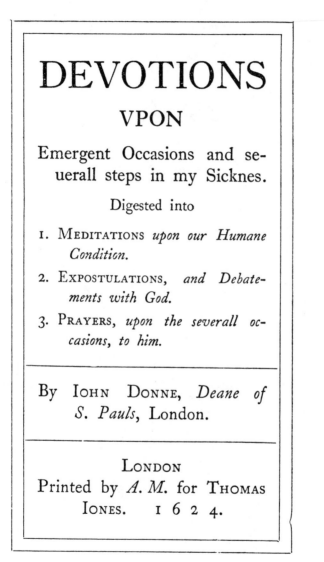

DEVOTIONS

VPON

Emergent Occasions and se-
uerall steps in my Sicknes.

Digested into

1. MEDITATIONS *upon our Humane
   Condition.*
2. EXPOSTULATIONS, *and Debate-
   ments with God.*
3. PRAYERS, *upon the severall occasions, to him.*

By IOHN DONNE, *Deane of
S. Pauls*, London.

LONDON
Printed by *A. M.* for THOMAS
IONES.   1 6 2 4.

TO THE MOST EXCELLENT PRINCE,

PRINCE CHARLES.

MOST EXCELLENT PRINCE,

I HAVE had three births; one, natural, when I came into the world; one, supernatural, when I entered into the ministry; and now, a preternatural birth, in returning to life, from this sickness. In my second birth, your Highness' royal father vouchsafed me his hand, not only to sustain me in it, but to lead me to it. In this last birth, I myself am born a father: this child of mine, this book, comes into the world, from me, and with me. And therefore, I presume (as I did the father, to the Father) to present the son to the Son; this image of my humiliation, to the lively image of his Majesty, your Highness. It might be enough, that God hath seen my devotions: but examples of good kings are commandments; and Hezekiah writ the meditations of his sickness, after his sickness. Besides, as I have lived to see (not as a witness only, but as a partaker), the happiness of a part of your royal father's time, so shall I live (in my way) to see the happiness of the times of your Highness too, if this child of mine, inanimated by your gracious acceptation, may so long preserve alive the memory of

Your Highness humblest and devotedest,

JOHN DONNE.

3

CONTENTS

The Stations of the Sickness

DEVOTIONS

The first Alteration, the first Grudging, of the Sickness.

I. MEDITATION.

VARIABLE, and therefore miserable condition of
man! this minute I was well, and am ill, this minute.
I am surprised with a sudden change, and alteration
to worse, and can impute it to no cause, nor call it by any
name. We study health, and we deliberate upon our
meats, and drink, and air, and exercises, and we hew and
we polish every stone that goes to that building; and so
our health is a long and a regular work: but in a minute
a cannon batters all, overthrows all, demolishes all; a
sickness unprevented for all our diligence, unsuspected
for all our curiosity; nay, undeserved, if we consider only

disorder, summons us, seizes us, possesses us, destroys us
in an instant. O miserable condition of man! which was
not imprinted by God, who, as he is immortal himself,
had put a coal, a beam of immortality into us, which we
might have blown into a flame, but blew it out by our
first sin; we beggared ourselves by hearkening after false
riches, and infatuated ourselves by hearkening after false
knowledge. So that now, we do not only die, but die
upon the rack, die by the torment of sickness; nor that
only, but are pre-afflicted, super-afflicted with these
jealousies and suspicions and apprehensions of sickness,
before we can call it a sickness: we are not sure we are
ill; one hand asks the other by the pulse, and our eye asks
our own urine how we do. O multiplied misery! we die,
and cannot enjoy death, because we die in this torment of
sickness; we are tormented with sickness, and cannot
stay till the torment come, but pre-apprehensions and
presages prophesy those torments which induce that
death before either come; and our dissolution is conceived
in these first changes, quickened in the sickness itself, and
born in death, which bears date from these first changes.
Is this the honour which man hath by being a little world,
that he hath these earthquakes in himself, sudden shakings;
these lightnings, sudden flashes; these thunders, sudden
noises; these eclipses, sudden offuscations and darkening
of his senses; these blazing stars, sudden fiery exhalations;
these rivers of blood, sudden red waters? Is he a world
to himself only therefore, that he hath enough in himself,
not only to destroy and execute himself, but to presage
that execution upon himself; to assist the sickness, to
antedate the sickness, to make the sickness the more
irremediable by sad apprehensions, and, as if he would
make a fire the more vehement by sprinkling water upon
the coals, so to wrap a hot fever in cold melancholy, lest

8

the fever alone should not destroy fast enough without this contribution, nor perfect the work (which is destruction) except we joined an artificial sickness of our own melancholy, to our natural, our unnatural fever. O perplexed discomposition, O riddling distemper, O miserable condition of man!

I. EXPOSTULATION.

IF I were but mere dust and ashes I might speak unto the Lord, for the Lord's hand made me of this dust, and the Lord's hand shall re-collect these ashes; the Lord's hand was the wheel upon which this vessel of clay was framed, and the Lord's hand is the urn in which these ashes shall be preserved. I am the dust and the ashes of the temple of the Holy Ghost, and what marble is so precious? But I am more than dust and ashes: I am my best part, I am my soul. And being so, the breath of God, I may breathe back these pious expostulations to my God: My God, my God, why is not my soul as sensible as my body? Why hath not my soul these apprehensions, these presages, these changes, these antidates, these jealousies, these suspicions of a sin, as well as my body of a sickness? Why is there not always a pulse in my soul to beat at the approach of a temptation to sin? Why are there not always waters in mine eyes, to testify my spiritual sickness? I stand in the way of temptations, naturally, necessarily; all men do so; for there is a snake in every path, temptations in every vocation; but I go, I run, I fly into the ways of temptation which I might shun; nay, I break into houses where the plague is; I press into places of temptation, and tempt the devil himself, and solicit and importune them who had rather be left unsolicited by me. I fall sick of sin, and am bedded and bedrid, buried and putrified in the practice of sin, and all this while have no presage, no pulse, no sense of my sickness. O height, O depth of misery, where the first symptom of the sickness is hell, and where I never see the fever of lust, of envy, of ambition, by any other light than the darkness and horror of hell itself, and where the first messenger that speaks to me doth not say, " Thou mayest die," no, nor " Thou must die," but " Thou art dead; " and where the first notice that my soul hath of her sickness is irrecoverableness, irremediableness: but, O my God, Job did not charge thee foolishly in his temporal afflictions, nor may I in my spiritual. Thou hast imprinted a pulse in our soul, but we do not examine it; a voice in our conscience, but we do not hearken unto it. We talk it out, we jest it out, we drink it out, we sleep it out; and when we wake, we do not say with Jacob, *Surely the Lord is in this place, and I knew it not:* but though we might know it, we do not, we will not. But will God pretend to make a watch, and leave out the spring? to make so many various wheels in the faculties of the soul, and in the organs of the body, and leave out grace, that should move them? or will God make a spring, and not wind it up? Infuse his first grace, and not second it with more, without which we can no more use his first grace when we have it, than we could dispose ourselves by nature to have it? But alas, that is not our case; we are all prodigal sons, and not disinherited; we have received our portion, and mispent it, not been denied it. We are God's tenants here, and yet here, he, our landlord, pays us rents; not yearly, nor quarterly, but hourly, and quarterly; every minute he renews his mercy, but we *will not understand, lest that we should be converted, and he should heal us.*[1]

---

[1] Matt. xiii. 16.

I. PRAYER.

O ETERNAL and most gracious God, who, considered in thyself, art a circle, first and last, and altogether; but, considered in thy working upon us, art a direct line, and leadest us from our beginning, through all our ways, to our end, enable me by thy grace to look forward to mine end, and to look backward too, to the considerations of thy mercies afforded me from the beginning; that so by that practice of considering thy mercy, in my beginning in this world, when thou plantedst me in the Christian church, and thy mercy in the beginning in the other world, when thou writest me in the book of life, in my election, I may come to a holy consideration of thy mercy in the beginning of all my actions here: that in all the beginnings, in all the accesses and approaches, of spiritual sicknesses of sin, I may hear and hearken to that voice, *O thou man of God, there is death in the pot,*[2] and so refrain from that which I was so hungerly, so greedily flying to. *A faithful ambassador is health,*[3] says thy wise servant Solomon. Thy voice received in the beginning of a sickness, of a sin, is true health. If I can see that light betimes, and hear that voice early, *Then shall my light break forth as the morning, and my health shall spring forth speedily.*[4] Deliver me therefore, O my God, from these vain imaginations; that it is an over-curious thing, a dangerous thing, to come to that tenderness, that rawness, that scrupulousness, to fear every concupiscence, every offer of sin, that this suspicious and jealous diligence will turn to an inordinate dejection of spirit, and a diffidence in thy care and providence; but keep

[2] 2 Kings, iv. 40.   [3] Prov. xiii. 17.
[4] Isaiah, lviii. 8.

11

me still established, both in a constant assurance, that thou wilt speak to me at the beginning of every such sickness, at the approach of every such sin; and that, if I take knowledge of that voice then, and fly to thee, thou wilt preserve me from falling, or raise me again, when by natural infirmity I am fallen. Do this, O Lord, for his sake, who knows our natural infirmities, for he had them, and knows the weight of our sins, for he paid a dear price for them, thy Son, our Saviour, Christ Jesus. Amen.

II. POST ACTIO LÆSA.

The Strength and the function of the senses, and other faculties, change and fail.

II. MEDITATION.

THE heavens are not the less constant, because they move continually, because they move continually one and the same way. The earth is not the more constant, because it lies still continually, because continually it changes and melts in all the parts thereof. Man, who is the noblest part of the earth, melts so away, as if he were a statue, not of earth, but of snow. We see his own envy melts him, he grows lean with that; he will say, another's beauty melts him; but he feels that a fever doth not melt him like snow, but pour him out like lead, like iron, like brass melted in a furnace; it doth not only melt him, but calcine him, reduce him to atoms, and to ashes; not to water, but to lime. And how quickly? Sooner than thou canst receive an answer, sooner than thou canst conceive the question; earth is the centre of my body, heaven is the centre of my soul; these two are

12

the natural places of these two; but those go not to these two in an equal pace: my body falls down without pushing; my soul does not go up without pulling; ascension is my soul's pace and measure, but precipitation my body's. And even angels, whose home is heaven, and who are winged too, yet had a ladder to go to heaven by steps. The sun which goes so many miles in a minute, the stars of the firmament which go so very many more, go not so fast as my body to the earth. In the same instant that I feel the first attempt of the disease, I feel the victory; in the twinkling of an eye I can scarce see; instantly the taste is insipid and fatuous; instantly the appetite is dull and desireless; instantly the knees are sinking and strengthless; and in an instant, sleep, which is the picture, the copy of death, is taken away, that the original, death itself, may succeed, and that so I might have death to the life. It was part of Adam's punishment, *In the sweat of thy brows thou shalt eat thy bread:* it is multiplied to me, I have earned bread in the sweat of my brows, in the labour of my calling, and I have it; and I sweat again and again, from the brow to the sole of the foot, but I eat no bread, I taste no sustenance: miserable distribution of mankind, where one half lacks meat, and the other stomach!

II. EXPOSTULATION.

DAVID professes himself a dead dog to his king Saul,[1] and so doth Mephibosheth to his king David,[2] and yet David speaks to Saul, and Mephibosheth to David. No man is so little, in respect of the greatest man, as the greatest in respect of God; for here, in that,

[1] 1 Sam. xxiv. 15.   [2] 2 Sam. ix. 8.

we have not so much as a measure to try it by; proportion is no measure for infinity. He that hath no more of this world but a grave; he that hath his grave but lent him till a better man or another man must be buried in the same grave; he that hath no grave but a dunghill, he that hath no more earth but that which he carries, but that which he is, he that hath not that earth which he is, but even in that is another's slave, hath as much proportion to God, as if all David's worthies, and all the world's monarchs, and all imagination's giants, were kneaded and incorporated into one, and as though that one were the survivor of all the sons of men, to whom God had given the world. And therefore how little soever I be, as *God calls things that are not, as though they were*, I, who am as though I were not, may call upon God, and say, My God, my God, why comes thine anger so fast upon me? Why dost thou melt me, scatter me, pour me like water upon the ground so instantly? Thou stayedst for the first world, in Noah's time, one hundred and twenty years; thou stayedst for a rebellious generation in the wilderness forty years, wilt thou stay no minute for me? Wilt thou make thy process and thy decree, thy citation and thy judgment, but one act? Thy summons, thy battle, thy victory, thy triumph, all but one act; and lead me captive, nay, deliver me captive to death, as soon as thou declarest me to be enemy, and so cut me off even with the drawing of thy sword out of the scabbard, and for that question, How long was he sick? leave no other answer, but that the hand of death pressed upon him from the first minute? My God, my God, thou wast not wont to come in whirlwinds, but in soft and gentle air. Thy first breath breathed a soul into me, and shall thy breath blow it out? Thy breath in the congregation, thy word in the church, breathes com-

14

munion and consolation here, and consummation here-after; shall thy breath in this chamber breathe dissolution and destruction, divorce and separation? Surely it is not thou, it is not thy hand. The devouring sword, the consuming fire, the winds from the wilderness, the diseases of the body, all that afflicted Job, were from the hands of Satan; it is not thou. It is thou, thou my God, who hast led me so continually with thy hand, from the hand of my nurse, as that I know thou wilt not correct me, but with thine own hand. My parents would not give me over to a servant's correction, nor my God to Satan's. I am *fallen into the hands of God* with David, and with David I see that his mercies are great.[3] For by that mercy, I consider in my present state, not the haste and the despatch of the disease, in dissolving this body, so much as the much more haste and despatch, which my God shall use, in re-collecting and re-uniting this dust again at the resurrection. Then I shall hear his angels proclaim the *Surgite mortui*, Rise, ye dead. Though I be dead, I shall hear the voice; the sounding of the voice and the working of the voice shall be all one; and all shall rise there in a less minute than any one dies here.

II. PRAYER.

O MOST gracious God, who pursuest and perfectest thine own purposes, and dost not only remember me, by the first accesses of this sickness, that I must die, but inform me, by this further proceeding therein, that I may die now; who hast not only waked me with the first, but called me up, by casting me further down, and clothed me with thyself, by stripping me of my

[3] 2 Sam. xxiv. 14.

self, and by dulling my bodily senses to the meats and eases of this world, hast whet and sharpened my spiritual senses to the apprehension of thee; by what steps and degrees soever it shall please thee to go, in the dissolution of this body, hasten, O Lord, that pace, and multiply, O my God, those degrees, in the exaltation of my soul toward thee now, and to thee then. My taste is not gone away, but gone up to sit at David's table, *to taste, and see, that the Lord is good.*[4]   My stomach is not gone, but gone up, so far upwards toward the *supper of the Lamb*, with thy saints in heaven, as to the table, to the communion of thy saints here in earth. My knees are weak, but weak therefore that I should easily fall to and fix myself long upon my devotions to thee. *A sound heart is the life of the flesh;*[5] and a heart visited by thee, and directed to thee, by that visitation is a sound heart. *There is no soundness in my flesh, because of thine anger.*[6]   Interpret thine own work, and call this sickness correction, and not anger, and there is soundness in my flesh. *There is no rest in my bones, because of my sin;*[7] transfer my sins, with which thou art so displeased, upon him with whom thou art so well pleased, Christ Jesus, and there will be rest in my bones.   And, O my God, who madest thyself a light in a bush, in the midst of these brambles and thorns of a sharp sickness, appear unto me so that I may see thee, and know thee to be my God, applying thyself to me, even in these sharp and thorny passages.   Do this, O Lord, for his sake, who was not the less the King of heaven for thy suffering him to be crowned with thorns in this world.

[4] Psalm xxxiv. 8.   [5] Prov. xiv. 30.
[6] Psalm xxxviii. 3.   [7] Psalm xxxviii. 3.

III. Decubitus sequitur tandem.

The patient takes his bed.

III. MEDITATION.

WE attribute but one privilege and advantage to man's body above other moving creatures, that he is not, as others, grovelling, but of an erect, of an upright, form naturally built and disposed to the contemplation of heaven. Indeed it is a thankful form, and recompenses that soul, which gives it, with carrying that soul so many feet higher towards heaven. Other creatures look to the earth; and even that is no unfit object, no unfit contemplation for man, for thither he must come; but because man is not to stay there, as other creatures are, man in his natural form is carried to the contemplation of that place which is his home, heaven. This is man's prerogative; but what state hath he in this dignity? A fever can fillip him down, a fever can depose him; a fever can bring that head, which yesterday carried a crown of gold five feet towards a crown of glory, as low as his own foot to-day. When God came to breathe into man the breath of life, he found him flat upon the ground; when he comes to withdraw that breath from him again, he prepares him to it by laying him flat upon his bed. Scarce any prison so close that affords not the prisoner two or three steps. The anchorites that barked themselves up in hollow trees and immured themselves in hollow walls, that perverse man that barrelled himself in a tub, all could stand or sit, and enjoy some change of posture. A sick bed is a grave, and all that the patient

17

says there is but a varying of his own epitaph. Every night's bed is a type of the grave; at night we tell our servants at what hour we will rise, here we cannot tell ourselves at what day, what week, what month. Here the head lies as low as the foot; the head of the people as low as they whom those feet trod upon; and that hand that signed pardons is too weak to beg his own, if he might have it for lifting up that hand. Strange fetters to the feet, strange manacles to the hands, when the feet and hands are bound so much the faster, by how much the cords are slacker; so much the less able to do their offices, by how much more the sinews and ligaments are the looser. In the grave I may speak through the stones, in the voice of my friends, and in the accents of those words which their love may afford my memory; here I am mine own ghost, and rather affright my beholders than instruct them; they conceive the worst of me now, and yet fear worse; they give me for dead now, and yet wonder how I do when they wake at midnight, and ask how I do to-morrow. Miserable, and (though common to all) inhuman posture, where I must practise my lying in the grave by lying still, and not practise my resurrection by rising any more.

III. EXPOSTULATION.

M Y God and my Jesus, my Lord and my Christ, my strength and my salvation, I hear thee, and I hearken to thee, when thou rebukest thy disciples, for rebuking them who brought children to thee; *Suffer little children to come to me*, sayest thou.[8] Is there a verier child than I am now? I cannot say, with thy

[8] Matt. xix. 13.

servant Jeremy, *Lord, I am a child, and cannot speak;* but, O Lord, I am a sucking child, and cannot eat; a creeping child, and cannot go; how shall I come to thee? Whither shall I come to thee? To this bed? I have this weak and childish frowardness too, I cannot sit up, and yet am loth to go to bed. Shall I find thee in bed? Oh, have I always done so? The bed is not ordinarily thy scene, thy climate: Lord, dost thou not accuse me, dost thou not reproach to me my former sins, when thou layest me upon this bed? Is not this to hang a man at his own door, to lay him sick in his own bed of wantonness? When thou chidest us by thy prophet for lying in *beds of ivory*[9], is not thine anger vented; not till thou changest our beds of ivory into beds of ebony? David swears unto thee, *that he will not go up into his bed, till he had built thee a house.*[10] To go up into the bed denotes strength, and promises ease; but when thou sayest, *that thou wilt cast Jezebel into a bed,* thou makest thine own comment upon that; thou callest the bed tribulation, great tribulation.[11] How shall they come to thee whom thou hast nailed to their bed? Thou art in the congregation, and I in a solitude: when the centurion's servant lay sick at home,[12] his master was fain to come to Christ; the sick man could not. Their friend lay sick of the palsy, and the four charitable men were fain to bring him to Christ; he could not come.[13] Peter's wife's mother lay sick of a fever, and Christ came to her; she could not come to him.[14] My friends may carry me home to thee, in their prayers in the congregation; thou must come home to me in the visitation of thy Spirit, and in the seal of thy sacrament. But when I am cast into this bed my slack sinews are iron fetters, and those thin sheets

---

[9] Amos vi. 4.   [10] Psalm cxxxii. 3.   [11] Rev. ii. 22.
[12] Matt. viii. 6.   [13] Matt. viii. 4.   [14] Matt. viii. 14.

iron doors upon me; and, *Lord, I have loved the habitation of thine house, and the place where thine honour dwelleth.*[15] I lie here and say, *Blessed are they that dwell in thy house;*[16] but I cannot say, *I will come into thy house;* I may say, *In thy fear will I worship towards thy holy temple;*[17] but I cannot say in thy holy temple . And, *Lord, the zeal of thy house eats me up,*[18] as fast as my fever; it is not a recusancy, for I would come, but it is an excommunication, I must not. But, Lord, thou art Lord of hosts, and lovest action; why callest thou me from my calling? *In the grave no man shall praise thee;* in the door of the grave, this sick bed, no man shall hear me praise thee. Thou hast not opened my lips that my mouth might show thee thy praise, but that my mouth might show forth thy praise. But thine apostle's fear takes hold of me, *that when I have preached to others, I myself should be a castaway;*[19] and therefore am I cast down, that I might not be cast away. Thou couldst take me by the head, as thou didst Habbakuk, and carry me so; by a chariot, as thou didst Elijah,[20] and carry me so; but thou carriest me thine own private way, the way by which thou carriedst thy Son, who first lay upon the earth and prayed, and then had his exaltation, as himself calls his crucifying; and first descended into hell, and then had his ascension. There is another station (indeed neither are stations but prostrations) lower than this bed; to-morrow I may be laid one story lower, upon the floor, the face of the earth; and next day another story, in the grave, the womb of the earth. As yet God suspends me between heaven and earth, as a meteor; and I am not in heaven because an earthly body clogs

---

[15] Psalm xxvi. 8. [16] Psalm lxxxiv. 4.
[17] Psalm v. 7.   [18] Psalm lxix. 9.
[19] 1 Cor. ix. 27.i [20] 2 Kngs, ii. 11.

me, and I am not in the earth because a heavenly soul sustains me. And it is thine own law, O God, that *if a man be smitten so by another, as that he keep his bed, though he die not, he that hurt him must take care of his healing, and recompense him*[21]. Thy hand strikes me into this bed; and therefore, if I rise again, thou wilt be my recompense all the days of my life, in making the memory of this sickness beneficial to me; and if my body fall yet lower, thou wilt take my soul out of this bath, and present it to thy Father, washed again, and again, and again, in thine own tears, in thine own sweat, in thine own blood.

III. PRAYER.

O MOST mighty and most merciful God, who, though thou have taken me off of my feet, hast not taken me off of my foundation, which is thyself; who, though thou have removed me from that upright form in which I could stand and see thy throne, the heavens, yet hast not removed from me that light by which I can lie and see thyself; who, though thou have weakened my bodily knees, that they cannot bow to thee, hast yet left me the knees of my heart; which are bowed unto thee evermore; as thou hast made this bed thine altar, make me thy sacrifice; and as thou makest thy Son Christ Jesus the priest, so make me his deacon, to minister to him in a cheerful surrender of my body and soul to thy pleasure, by his hands. I come unto thee, O God, my God, I come unto thee, so as I can come, I come to thee, by embracing thy coming to me, I come in the confidence, and in the application of thy servant David's promise,

[21] Exodus xxi. 18.

that thou wilt make all my bed in my sickness;[22] all my bed; that which way soever I turn, I may turn to thee; and as I feel thy hand upon all my body, so I may find it upon all my bed, and see all my corrections, and all my refreshings to flow from one and the same, and all from thy hand.   As thou hast made these feathers thorns, in the sharpness of this sickness, so, Lord, make these thorns feathers again, feathers of thy dove, in the peace of conscience, and in a holy recourse to thine ark, to the instruments of true comfort, in thy institutions and in the ordinances of thy church.   Forget my bed, O Lord, as it hath been a bed of sloth, and worse than sloth; take me not, O Lord, at this advantage, to terrify my soul with saying, Now I have met thee there where thou hast so often departed from me; but having burnt up that bed by these vehement heats, and washed that bed in these abundant sweats, make my bed again, O Lord, and enable me, according to thy command, *to commune with mine own heart upon my bed, and be still*[23]; to provide a bed for all my former sins whilst I lie upon this bed, and a grave for my sins before I come to my grave; and when I have deposited them in the wounds of thy Son, to rest in that assurance, that my conscience is discharged from further anxiety, and my soul from further danger, and my memory from further calumny.   Do this, O Lord, for his sake, who did and suffered so much, that thou mightest, as well in thy justice as in thy mercy, do it for me, thy Son, our Saviour, Christ Jesus.

[22] Psalm xli. 3.   [23] Psalm iv. 4.

IV. MEDICUSQUE VOCATUR.

The physician is sent for.

IV. MEDITATION.

IT is too little to call man a little world; except God, man is a diminutive to nothing. Man consists of more pieces, more parts, than the world; than the world doth, nay, than the world is. And if those pieces were extended, and stretched out in man as they are in the world, man would be the giant, and the world the dwarf; the world but the map, and the man the world. If all the veins in our bodies were extended to rivers, and all the sinews to veins of mines, and all the muscles that lie upon one another, to hills, and all the bones to quarries of stones, and all the other pieces to the proportion of those which correspond to them in the world, the air would be too little for this orb of man to move in, the firmament would be but enough for this star; for, as the whole world hath nothing, to which something in man doth not answer, so hath man many pieces of which the whole world hath no representation. Enlarge this meditation upon this great world, man, so far as to consider the immensity of the creatures this world produces; our creatures are our thoughts, creatures that are born giants; that reach from east to west, from earth to heaven; that do not only bestride all the sea and land, but span the sun and firmament at once; my thoughts reach all, comprehend all. Inexplicable mystery; I their creator am in a close prison, in a sick bed, any where, and any one of my creatures, my thoughts, is with the sun, and beyond the sun, overtakes the sun, and overgoes the sun in one pace, one step, everywhere. And then, as the other world produces serpents and vipers, malignant and venomous creatures, and worms and caterpillars, that endeavour to devour that world which produces them, and monsters compiled and complicated of divers parents and kinds; so this world, ourselves, produces all these in us, in producing diseases, and sicknesses of all those sorts: venomous and infectious diseases, feeding and consuming diseases, and manifold and entangled diseases made up of many several ones. And can the other world name so many venomous, so many consuming, so many monstrous creatures, as we can diseases of all these kinds? O miserable abundance, O beggarly riches! how much do we lack of having remedies for every disease, when as yet we have not names for them? But we have a Hercules against these giants, these monsters; that is, the physician; he musters up all the forces of the other world to succour this, all nature to relieve man. We have the physician, but we are not the physician. Here we shrink in our proportion, sink in our dignity, in respect of very mean creatures, who are physicians to themselves. The hart that is pursued and wounded, they say, knows an herb, which being eaten throws off the arrow: a strange kind of vomit. The dog that pursues it, though he be subject to sickness, even proverbially, knows his grass that recovers him. And it may be true, that the drugger is as near to man as to other creatures; it may be that obvious and present simples, easy to be had, would cure him; but the apothecary is not so near him, nor the physician so near him, as they two are to other creatures; man hath not that innate instinct, to apply those natural medicines to his present danger, as those inferior creatures have; he is not his own apothecary, his own physician, as they are. Call back therefore thy meditation again, and bring it down: what's become of

24

man's great extent and proportion, when himself shrinks himself and consumes himself to a handful of dust; what's become of his soaring thoughts, his compassing thoughts, when himself brings himself to the ignorance, to the thoughtlessness, of the grave? His diseases are his own, but the physician is not; he hath them at home, but he must send for the physician.

IV. EXPOSTULATION.

I HAVE not the righteousness of Job, but I have the desire of Job: *I would speak to the Almighty, and I would reason with God.*[1] My God, my God, how soon wouldst thou have me go to the physician, and how far wouldst thou have me go with the physician? I know thou hast made the matter, and the man, and the art; and I go not from thee when I go to the physician. Thou didst not make clothes before there was a shame of the nakedness of the body, but thou didst make physic before there was any grudging of any sickness; for thou didst imprint a medicinal virtue in many simples, even from the beginning; didst thou mean that we should be sick when thou didst so? when thou madest them? No more than thou didst mean, that we should sin, when thou madest us: thou foresawest both, but causedst neither. Thou, Lord, promisest here trees, *whose fruit shall be for meat, and their leaves for medicine.*[2] It is the voice of thy Son, *Wilt thou be made whole?*[3] that draws from the patient a confession that he was ill, and could not make himself well. And it is thine own voice, *Is there no physician?*[4] that inclines us, disposes us, to

---

[1] Job xiii. 3.   [2] Ezek. xlvii. 12.
[3] John v. 6.   [4] Jer. viii. 22.

25

accept thine ordinance. And it is the voice of the wise man, both for the matter, physic itself, *The Lord hath created medicines out of the earth, and he that is wise shall not abhor them,*[5] and for the art, and the person, the physician cutteth off a long disease. In all these voices thou sendest us to those helps which thou hast afforded us in that. But wilt not thou avow that voice too, *He that hath sinned against his Maker, let him fall into the hands of the physician;*[6] and wilt not thou afford me an understanding of those words? Thou, who sendest us for a blessing to the physician, dost not make it a curse to us to go when thou sendest. Is not the curse rather in this, that only he falls into the hands of the physician, that casts himself wholly, entirely upon the physician, confides in him, relies upon him, attends all from him, and neglects that spiritual physic which thou also hast instituted in thy church. So to fall into the hands of the physician is a sin, and a punishment of former sins; so, as Asa fell, who in his disease *sought not to the Lord, but to the physician.*[7] Reveal therefore to me thy method, O Lord, and see whether I have followed it; that thou mayest have glory, if I have, and I pardon, if I have not, and help that I may. Thy method is, *In time of thy sickness, be not negligent:* wherein wilt thou have my diligence expressed? *Pray unto the Lord, and he will make thee whole.*[8] O Lord, I do; I pray, and pray thy servant David's prayer, *Have mercy upon me, O Lord, for I am weak; heal me, O Lord, for my bones are vexed:*[9] I know that even my weakness is a reason, a motive, to induce thy mercy, and my sickness an occasion of thy sending health. When art thou so ready, when is it so seasonable to thee, to commiserate, as in misery? But

[5] Ecclus. xxxviii. 4. [6] Ecclus. xxxviii. 15.
[7] 1 Chron. xvi. 12. [8] Ecclus. xxxviii. 9.

is prayer for health in season, as soon as I am sick? Thy method goes further: *Leave off from sin, and order thy hands aright, and cleanse thy heart from all wickedness.*[10] Have I, O Lord, done so? O Lord, I have; by thy grace, I am come to a holy detestation of my former sin. Is there any more? In thy method there is more: *Give a sweet savour, and a memorial of fine flour, and make a fat offering, as not being.*[11] And, Lord, by thy grace, I have done that, sacrificed a little of that little which thou lentest me, to them for whom thou lentest it: and now in thy method, and by thy steps, I am come to that, *Then give place to the physician, for the Lord hath created him; let him not go from thee, for thou hast need of him.*[12] I send for the physician, but I will hear him enter with those words of Peter, *Jesus Christ maketh thee whole;*[13] I long for his presence, but I look *that the power of the Lord should be present to heal me.*[14]

IV.   PRAYER.

O MOST mighty and most merciful God, who art so the God of health and strength, as that without thee all health is but the fuel, and all strength but the bellows of sin; behold me under the vehemence of two diseases, and under the necessity of two physicians, authorized by thee, the bodily, and the spiritual physician. I come to both as to thine ordinance, and bless and glorify thy name that, in both cases, thou hast afforded help to man by the ministry of man. Even in the new Jerusalem, in heaven itself, it hath pleased thee to discover a tree,

---

[9] Psalm vi. 2.   [10] Ecclus. xxxviii. 10.
[11] Ecclus. xxxviii. 11.   [12] Ecclus. xxxviii. 12.
[13] Acts, ix. 34.   [14] Luke, v. 17.

which is *a tree of life there, but the leaves thereof are for the healing of the nations.*[15]   Life itself is with thee there, for thou art life; and all kinds of health, wrought upon us here by thine instruments, descend from thence.   *Thou wouldst have healed Babylon, but she is not healed.*[16]   Take from me, O Lord, her perverseness, her wilfulness, her refractoriness, and hear thy Spirit saying in my soul: Heal me, O Lord, for I would be healed.   *Ephraim saw his sickness, and Judah his wound; then went Ephraim to the Assyrian, and sent to King Jareb, yet could not he heal you, nor cure you of your wound.*[17]   Keep me back, O Lord, from them who misprofess arts of healing the soul, or of the body, by means not imprinted by thee in the church for the soul, or not in nature for the body.   There is no spiritual health to be had by superstition, nor bodily by witchcraft; thou, Lord, and only thou, art Lord of both. Thou in thyself art Lord of both, and thou in thy Son art the physician, the applier of both.   *With his stripes we are healed,*[18] says the prophet there; there, before he was scourged, we were healed with his stripes; how much more shall I be healed now, now when that which he hath already suffered actually is actually and effectually applied to me?   Is there any thing incurable, upon which that balm drops?   Any vein so empty as that that blood cannot fill it?   Thou promisest to heal the earth;[19] but it is when the inhabitants of the earth *pray that thou wouldst heal it.*   Thou promisest to heal their waters, but *their miry places and standing waters,* thou sayest there, *thou wilt not heal.*[20]   My returning to any sin, if I should return to the ability of sinning over all my sins again, thou wouldst not pardon.   Heal this earth, O my God, by repentant tears, and heal these waters, these tears,

---

[15] Rev. xxii. 2.   [16] Jer. li. 9.   [17] Hosea, v. 13.
[18] Isaiah, liii. 5.   [19] 2 Chron. vii. 14.   [20] Ezek. xlvii. 11.

from all bitterness, from all diffidence, from all dejection, by establishing my irremovable assurance in thee. *Thy Son went about healing all manner of sickness.*[21] (No disease incurable, none difficult; he healed them in passing). *Virtue went out of him, and he healed all,*[22] all the multitude (no person incurable), he healed them *every whit*[23] (as himself speaks), he left no relics of the disease; and will this universal physician pass by this hospital, and not visit me? not heal me? not heal me wholly? Lord, I look not that thou shouldst say by thy messenger to me, as to Hezekiah, *Behold, I will heal thee, and on the third day thou shalt go up to the house of the Lord.*[24] I look not that thou shouldst say to me, as to Moses in Miriam's behalf, when Moses would have had her healed presently, *If her father had but spit in her face, should she not have been ashamed seven days? Let her be shut up seven days, and then return;*[25] but if thou be pleased to multiply seven days (and seven is infinite) by the number of my sins (and that is more infinite), if this day must remove me till days shall be no more, seal to me my spiritual health, in affording me the seals of thy church; and for my temporal health, prosper thine ordinance, in their hands who shall assist in this sickness, in that manner, and in that measure, as may most glorify thee, and most edify those who observe the issues of thy servants, to their own spiritual benefit.

[21] Matt. iv. 23. [22] Luke, vi. 19. [23] John, vii. 23.
[24] 2 Kings, xx. 5. [25] Num. xii. 14.

V. SOLUS ADEST.

The physician comes

V. MEDITATION.

AS sickness is the greatest misery, so the greatest misery of sickness is solitude; when the infectiousness of the disease deters them who should assist from coming; even the physician dares scarce come. Solitude is a torment which is not threatened in hell itself. Mere vacuity, the first agent, God, the first instrument of God, nature, will not admit; nothing can be utterly empty, but so near a degree towards vacuity as solitude, to be but one, they love not. When I am dead, and my body might infect, they have a remedy, they may bury me; but when I am but sick, and might infect, they have no remedy but their absence, and my solitude. It is an excuse to them that are great, and pretend, and yet are loath to come; it is an inhibition to those who would truly come, because they may be made instruments, and pestiducts, to the infection of others, by their coming. And it is an outlawry, an excommunication upon the patient, and separates him from all offices, not only of civility but of working charity. A long sickness will weary friends at last, but a pestilential sickness averts them from the beginning. God himself would admit a figure of society, as there is a plurality of persons in God, though there be but one God; and all his external actions testify a love of society, and communion. In heaven there are orders of angels, and armies of martyrs, and in that house many mansions; in earth, families, cities, churches, colleges, all plural things; and lest either of these should not be company enough alone, there is an

30

association of both, a communion of saints which makes the militant and triumphant church one parish; so that Christ was not out of his diocess when he was upon the earth, nor out of his temple when he was in our flesh. God, who saw that all that he made was good, came not so near seeing a defect in any of his works, as when he saw that it was not good for man to be alone, therefore he made him a helper; and one that should help him so as to increase the number, and give him her own, and more society. Angels, who do not propagate nor multiply, were made at first in an abundant number, and so were stars; but for the things of this world, their blessing was, Increase; for I think, I need not ask leave to think, that there is no phœnix; nothing singular, nothing alone. Men that inhere upon nature only, are so far from thinking that there is any thing singular in this world, as that they will scarce think that this world itself is singular, but that every planet, and every star, is another world like this; they find reason to conceive not only a plurality in every species in the world, but a plurality of worlds; so that the abhorrers of solitude are not solitary, for God, and Nature, and Reason concur against it. Now a man may counterfeit the plague in a vow, and mistake a disease for religion, by such a retiring and recluding of himself from all men as to do good to no man, to converse with no man. God hath two testaments, two wills; but this is a schedule, and not of his, a codicil, and not of his, not in the body of his testaments, but interlined and postscribed by others, that the way to the communion of saints should be by such a solitude as excludes all doing of good here. That is a disease of the mind, as the height of an infectious disease of the body is solitude, to be left alone: for this makes an infectious bed equal, nay, worse than a grave, that though in both I be equally alone, in my bed I know it, and feel it, and shall not in my grave: and this too, that in my bed my soul is still in an infectious body, and shall not in my grave be so.

V. EXPOSTULATION.

O GOD, my God, thy Son took it not ill at Martha's hands, that when he said unto her, *Thy brother Lazarus shall rise again,*[1] she expostulated it so far with him as to reply, *I know that he shall rise again in the resurrection, at the last day;* for she was miserable by wanting him then. Take it not ill, O my God, from me, that though thou have ordained it for a blessing, and for a dignity to thy people, *that they should dwell alone, and not be reckoned among the nations*[2] (because they should be above them), and that *they should dwell in safety alone*[3] (free from the infestation of enemies), yet I take thy leave to remember thee, that thou hast said too, *Two are better than one;* and, *Woe be unto him that is alone when he falleth;*[4] and so when he is fallen, and laid in the bed of sickness too. *Righteousness is immortal;*[5] I know thy wisdom hath said so; but no man, though covered with the righteousness of thy Son, is immortal so as not to die; for he who was righteousness itself did die. I know that the Son of Righteousness, thy Son, refused not, nay affected, solitariness, loneness,[6] many, many times; but at all times he was able to command *more than twelve legions of angels*[7] to his service; and when he did not so, he was far from being alone: for, *I am not alone,* says he, *but I, and the Father that sent me.*[8] I cannot fear but that I

---

[1] John, xi. 23.   [2] Num. xxiii. 9.   [3] Deut. xxxiii. 28.
[4] Eccles. iv. 10.   [5] Wisd. i. 15.   [6] Matt. xiv. 23.
[7] Matt. xxvi. 13.   [8] John, viii. 16.

shall always be with thee and him; but whether this disease may not alien and remove my friends, so that *they stand aloof from my sore, and my kinsmen stand afar off*,[9] I cannot tell. I cannot fear but that thou wilt reckon with me from this minute, in which, by thy grace, I see thee; whether this understanding, and this will, and this memory may not decay, to the discouragement and the ill interpretation of them that see that heavy change in me, I cannot tell. It was for thy blessed, thy powerful Son alone, *to tread the wine-press alone, and none of the people with him*.[10] I am not able to pass this agony alone, not alone without thee; thou art thy spirit, not alone without thine; spiritual and temporal physicians are thine, not alone without mine; those whom the bands of blood or friendship have made mine, are mine; and if thou, or thine, or mine, abandon me, I am alone, and woe unto me if I be alone. Elias himself fainted under that apprehension, *Lo, I am left alone*;[11] and Martha murmured at that, said to Christ, *Lord, dost not thou care that my sister hath left me to serve alone?*[12] Neither could Jeremiah enter into his lamentations from a higher ground than to say, *How doth the city sit solitary that was full of people.*[13] O my God, it is the leper that thou hast condemned to live alone;[14] have I such a leprosy in my soul that I must die alone; alone without thee? Shall this come to such a leprosy in my body that I must die alone; alone without them that should assist, that should comfort me? But comes not this expostulation too near a murmuring? Must I be concluded with that, that Moses *was commanded to come near the Lord alone*;[15] that solitariness, and dereliction, and abandoning of others, disposes us

---

.[9] Psalm xxxviii. 11.
[11] 1 Kings, xiv. 14.
[13] Jer. i. 1. [14] Lev. xiii. 46.
[10] Isaiah lxiii. 3.
[12] Luke, x. 40.
[15] Exod. xiv. 2.

best for God, who accompanies us most alone? May I
not remember, and apply too, that though God came not
to Jacob till he found him alone, yet when he found him
alone, he wrestled with him, and lamed him;[16] that
when, in the dereliction and forsaking of friends and
physicians, a man is left alone to God, God may so
wrestle with this Jacob, with this conscience, as to put it
out of joint, and so appear to him as that he dares not look
upon him face to face, when as by way of reflection, in
the consolation of his temporal or spiritual servants, and
ordinances he durst, if they were there? But a *faithful
friend is the physic of life, and they that fear the Lord shall
find him.*[17] Therefore hath the Lord afforded me both
in one person, that physician who is my faithful friend.

V. PRAYER.

O ETERNAL and most gracious God, who calledst
down fire from heaven upon the sinful cities but
once, and openedst the earth to swallow the mur-
murers but once, and threwest down the tower of Siloam
upon sinners but once; but for thy works of mercy
repeatedst them often, and still workest by thine own
patterns, as thou broughtest man into this world, by
giving him a helper fit for him here; so, whether it be thy
will to continue me long thus, or to dismiss me by death,
be pleased to afford me the helps fit for both conditions,
either for my weak stay here, or my final transmigration
from hence. And if thou mayst receive glory by that
way (and by all ways thou mayst receive glory), glorify
thyself in preserving this body from such infections as
might withhold those who would come, or endanger

[16] Gen. xxxii. 24. 25.   [17] Ecclus. vi. 16.

them who do come; and preserve this soul in the faculties thereof from all such distempers as might shake the assurance which myself and others have had, that because thou hast loved me thou wouldst love me to my end, and at my end. Open none of my doors, not of my heart, not of mine ears, not of my house, to any supplanter that would enter to undermine me in my religion to thee, in the time of my weakness, or to defame me, and magnify himself with false rumours of such a victory and surprisal of me, after I am dead. Be my salvation, and plead my salvation; work it and declare it; and as thy triumphant shall be, so let the militant church be assured that thou wast my God, and I thy servant, to and in my consummation. Bless thou the learning and the labours of this man whom thou sendest to assist me; and since thou takest me by the hand, and puttest me into his hands (for I come to him in thy name, who in thy name comes to me), since I clog not my hopes in him, no, nor my prayers to thee, with any limited conditions, but inwrap all in those two petitions, *Thy kingdom come, thy will be done*, prosper him, and relieve me, in thy way, in thy time, and in thy measure. Amen.

VI. METUIT.

The physician is afraid.

VI. MEDITATION.

I OBSERVE the physician with the same diligence as he the disease; I see he fears, and I fear with him; I overtake him, I overrun him, in his fear, and I go the faster, because he makes his pace slow; I fear the more, because he disguises his fear, and I see it with the more sharpness, because he would not have me see it. He knows that his fear shall not disorder the practice and exercise of his art, but he knows that my fear may disorder the effect and working of his practice. As the ill affections of the spleen complicate and mingle themselves with every infirmity of the body, so doth fear insinuate itself in every action or passion of the mind; and as wind in the body will counterfeit any disease, and seem the stone, and seem the gout, so fear will counterfeit any disease of the mind. It shall seem love, a love of having; and it is but a fear, a jealous and suspicious fear of losing. It shall seem valour in despising and undervaluing danger; and it is but fear in an overvaluing of opinion and estimation, and a fear of losing that. A man that is not afraid of a lion is afraid of a cat; not afraid of starving, and yet is afraid of some joint of meat at the table presented to feed him; not afraid of the sound of drums and trumpets and shot and those which they seek to drown, the last cries of men, and is afraid of some particular harmonious instrument; so much afraid as that with any of these the enemy might drive this man, otherwise valiant enough, out of the field. I know not what fear is, nor I know not what it is that I fear now; I fear not the hastening of my death, and yet I do fear the increase of the disease; I should belie nature if I should deny that I feared this; and if I should say that I feared death, I should belie God. My weakness is from nature, who hath but her measure; my strength is from God, who possesses and distributes infinitely. As then every cold air is not a damp, every shivering is not a stupefaction; so every fear is not a fearfulness, every declination is not a running away, every debating is not a resolving, every wish that it were not thus, is not a murmuring nor a dejection, though it be thus; but as my

36

physician's fear puts not him from his practice, neither doth mine put me from receiving from God, and man, and myself, spiritual and civil and moral assistances and consolations.

VI. EXPOSTULATION.

M Y God, my God, I find in thy book that fear is a stifling spirit, a spirit of suffocation; that *Ishbosheth could not speak, nor reply in his own defence to Abner, because he was afraid.*[1]   It was thy servant Job's case too, who, before he could say anything to thee, says of thee, *Let him take his rod away from me, and let not his fear terrify me, then would I speak with him, and not fear him; but it is not so with me.*[2]   Shall a fear of thee take away my devotion to thee?   Dost thou command me to speak to thee, and command me to fear thee; and do these destroy one another?   There is no perplexity in thee, my God; no inextricableness in thee, my light and my clearness, my sun and my moon, that directest me as well in the night of adversity and fear, as in my day of prosperity and confidence.   I must then speak to thee at all times, but when must I fear thee?   At all times too.   When didst thou rebuke any petitioner with the name of importunate?   Thou hast proposed to us a parable of a judge[3] that did justice at last, because the client was importunate, and troubled him; but thou hast told us plainly, that thy use in that parable was not that thou wast troubled with our importunities, but (as thou sayest there) *that we should always pray.*   And to the same purpose thou proposest another,[4] that if I press my friend, when he is in bed at

---

[1] 2 Sam. iii. 11.   [2] Job, ix. 34.
[3] Luke, xviii. 1.   [4] Luke, xi. 5.

midnight, to lend me bread, though he will not rise because I am his friend, yet because of mine importunity he will. God will do this whensoever thou askest, and never call it importunity. Pray in thy bed at midnight, and God will not say, I will hear thee to-morrow upon thy knees, at thy bedside; pray upon thy knees there then, and God will not say, I will hear thee on Sunday at church; God is no dilatory God, no froward God; prayer is never unseasonable, God is never asleep, nor absent. But, O my God, can I do this, and fear thee; come to thee and speak to thee, in all places, at all hours, and fear thee? Dare I ask this question? There is more boldness in the question than in the coming; I may do it though I fear thee; I cannot do it except I fear thee. So well hast thou provided that we should always fear thee, as that thou hast provided that we should fear no person but thee, nothing but thee; no men? No. Whom? *The Lord is my help and my salvation, whom shall I fear?*[5] Great enemies? Not great enemies, for no enemies are great to them that fear thee. *Fear not the people of this land, for they are bread to you;*[6] they shall not only not eat us, not eat our bread, but they shall be our bread. Why should we fear them? But for all this metaphorical bread, victory over enemies that thought to devour us, may we not fear, that we may lack bread literally? And fear famine, though we fear not enemies? *Young lions do lack and suffer hunger, but they that seek the Lord shall not want any good thing.*[7] Never? Though it be well with them at one time, may they not fear that it may be worse? *Wherefore should I fear in the days of evil?*[8] says thy servant David. Though his own sin had made them evil, he feared them not. No? not if

[5] Psalm xxvii. 1.   [6] Num. xiv. 9.
[7] Psalm xxxv. 70.   [8] Psalm xlix. 5.

this evil determine in death? Not though in a death; not though in a death inflicted by violence, by malice, by our own desert; *fear not the sentence of death,*[9] if thou fear God. Thou art, O my God, so far from admitting us that fear thee to fear others, as that thou makest others to fear us; as *Herod feared John, because he was a holy and a just man, and observed him.*[10] How fully then, O my abundant God, how gently, O my sweet, my easy God, dost thou unentangle me in any scruple arising out of the consideration of thy fear! Is not this that which thou intendest when thou sayest, *The secret of the Lord is with them that fear him;*[11] the secret, the mystery of the right use of fear. Dost thou not mean this when thou sayest, *we shall understand the fear of the Lord?*[12] Have it, and have benefit by it; have it, and stand under it; be directed by it, and not be dejected with it. And dost thou not propose that church for our example when thou sayest, the church of Judea *walked in the fear of God;*[13] they had it, but did not sit down lazily, nor fall down weakly, nor sink under it. There is a fear which weakens men in the service of God. *Adam was afraid, because he was naked.*[14] They who have put off thee are a prey to all. They may fear, for *Thou wilt laugh when their fear comes upon them,* as thou hast told them more than once.[15] And thou wilt make them fear where no cause of fear is, as thou hast told them more than once too.[16] There is a fear that is a punishment of former wickednesses, and induces more. Though some said of thy Son, Christ Jesus, *that he was a good man, yet no man spake openly for fear of the Jews.* Joseph was his disciple, *but secretly, for fear of the Jews.*[17]

[9] Ecclus. xli. 3.   [10] Mark, vi. 20.   [11] Psalm xxv. 14.
[12] Prov. ii. 5.   [13] Acts, ix. 31.   [14] Gen. iii. 10.
[15] Prov. i. 26; x. 24.   [16] Psalm xiv. 5; liii. 5.
[17] John, vii. 13; xix. 38; xxix. 19

The disciples kept some meetings, but with doors shut for fear of the Jews. O my God, thou givest us fear for ballast to carry us steadily in all weathers. But thou wouldst ballast us with such sand as should have gold in it, with that fear which is thy fear; for *the fear of the Lord is his treasure.*[18]   He that hath that lacks nothing that man can have, nothing that God does give. Timorous men thou rebukest: *Why are ye fearful, O ye of little faith?*[19] Such thou dismissest from thy service with scorn, though of them there went from Gideon's army twenty-two thousand, and remained but ten thousand.[20]   Such thou sendest farther than so; thither from whence they never return: *The fearful and the unbelieving, into that burning lake which is the second death.*[21]   There is a fear and there is a hope, which are equal abominations to thee; for, they were confounded because they hoped,[22] says thy servant Job; because they had misplaced, miscentred their hopes, they hoped, and not in thee, and such shall fear, and not fear thee. But in thy fear, my God, and my fear, my God, and my hope, is hope, and love, and confidence, and peace, and every limb and ingredient of happiness enwrapped; for joy includes all, and fear and joy consist together, nay, constitute one another. *The women departed from the sepulchre,*[23] the women who were made supernumerary apostles, apostles to the apostles; mothers of the church, and of the fathers, grandfathers of the church, the apostles themselves; the women, angels of the resurrection, went from the sepulchre with fear and joy; they ran, says the text, and they ran upon those two legs, fear and joy; and both was the right leg; they joy in thee, O Lord, that fear thee, and fear thee only, who feel this joy in thee. Nay, thy fear, and thy love are

[18] Isaiah, xxxiii. 6.   [19] Matt. viii. 26.   [20] Judges, vii. 3.
[21] Rev. xxi. 8.   [22] Job, vi. 20.   [23] Matt. xxviii. 8.

inseparable; still we are called upon, in infinite places, to fear God, yet the commandment, which is the root of all is, Thou shalt love the Lord thy God; he doeth neither that doeth not both; he omits neither, that does one. Therefore when thy servant David had said that *the fear of the Lord is the beginning of wisdom,*[24] and his son had repeated it again,[25] he that collects both calls this fear the root of wisdom; and, that it may embrace all, he calls it wisdom itself.[26] A wise man, therefore, is never without it, never without the exercise of it; therefore thou sentest Moses to thy people, *that they might learn to fear thee all the days of their lives,*[27] not in heavy and calamitous, but in good and cheerful days too; for Noah, who had assurance of his deliverance, yet, *moved with fear, prepared an ark, for the saving of his house.*[28] *A wise man will fear in everything.*[29] And therefore, though I pretend to no other degree of wisdom, I am abundantly rich in this, that I lie here possessed with that fear which is thy fear, both that this sickness is thy immediate correction, and not merely a natural accident, and therefore fearful, because it is a fearful thing to fall into thy hands; and that this fear preserves me from all inordinate fear, arising out of the infirmity of nature, because thy hand being upon me, thou wilt never let me fall out of thy hand.

VI. PRAYER.

O MOST mighty God, and merciful God, the God of all true sorrow, and true joy too, of all fear, and of all hope too, as thou hast given me a repentance, not to be repented of, so give me, O Lord, a fear, of which

[24] Psalm cxi. 10. [25] Prov. i. 7. [26] Ecclus. i. 20, 27.
[27] Deut. iv. 10. [28] Heb. xi. 7. [29] Ecclus. xviii. 27.

I may not be afraid. Give me tender and supple and conformable affections, that as I joy with them that joy, and mourn with them that mourn, so I may fear with them that fear. And since thou hast vouchsafed to discover to me, in his fear whom thou hast admitted to be my assistance in this sickness, that there is danger therein, let me not, O Lord, go about to overcome the sense of that fear, so far as to pretermit the fitting and preparing of myself for the worst that may be feared, the passage out of this life. Many of thy blessed martyrs have passed out of this life without any show of fear; but thy most blessed Son himself did not so. Thy martyrs were known to be but men, and therefore it pleased thee to fill them with thy Spirit and thy power, in that they did more than men; thy Son was declared by thee, and by himself, to be God; and it was requisite that he should declare himself to be man also, in the weaknesses of man. Let me not therefore, O my God, be ashamed of these fears, but let me feel them to determine where his fear did, in a present submitting of all to thy will. And when thou shalt have inflamed and thawed my former coldnesses and indevotions with these heats, and quenched my former heats with these sweats and inundations, and rectified my former presumptions and negligences with these fears, be pleased, O Lord, as one made so by thee, to think me fit for thee; and whether it be thy pleasure to dispose of this body, this garment, so as to put it to a farther wearing in this world, or to lay it up in the common wardrobe, the grave, for the next, glorify thyself in thy choice now, and glorify it then, with that glory, which thy Son, our Saviour Christ Jesus, hath purchased for them whom thou makest partakers of his resurrection. Amen.

VII. SOCIOS SIBI JUNGIER INSTAT.

The physician desires to have others joined with him.

VII. MEDITATION.

THERE is more fear, therefore more cause. If the physician desire help, the burden grows great: there is a growth of the disease then; but there must be an autumn too; but whether an autumn of the disease or me, it is not my part to choose; but if it be of me, it is of both; my disease cannot survive me, I may overlive it. Howsoever, his desiring of others argues his candour, and his ingenuity; if the danger be great, he justifies his proceedings, and he disguises nothing that calls in witnesses; and if the danger be not great, he is not ambitious, that is so ready to divide the thanks and the honour of that work which he begun alone, with others. It diminishes not the dignity of a monarch that he derive part of his care upon others; God hath not made many suns, but he hath made many bodies that receive and give light. The Romans began with one king; they came to two consuls; they returned in extremities to one dictator: whether in one or many, the sovereignty is the same in all states and the danger is not the more, and the providence is the more, where there are more physicians ; as the state is the happier where businesses are carried by more counsels than can be in one breast, how large soever. Diseases themselves hold consultations, and conspire how they may multiply, and join with one another, and exalt one another's force so; and shall we not call physicians to consultations? Death is in an old man's door, he appears and tells him so, and death is at a young man's back, and says nothing; age is a sickness,

43

and youth is an ambush; and we need so many physicians as may make up a watch, and spy every inconvenience. There is scarce any thing that hath not killed somebody; a hair, a feather hath done it; nay, that which is our best antidote against it hath done it; the best cordial hath been deadly posion. Men have died of joy, and almost forbidden their friends to weep for them, when they have seen them die laughing. Even that tyrant, Dionysius (I think the same that suffered so much after), who could not die of that sorrow, of that high fall, from a king to a wretched private man, died of so poor a joy as to be declared by the people at a theatre that he was a good poet. We say often that a man may live of a little; but, alas, of how much less may a man die? And therefore the more assistants the better. Who comes to a day of hearing, in a cause of any importance, with one advocate? In our funerals we ourselves have no interest; there we cannot advise, we cannot direct; and though some nations (the Egyptians in particular) built themselves better tombs than houses because they were to dwell longer in them, yet amongst ourselves, the greatest man of style whom we have had, the Conqueror, was left, as soon as his soul left him, not only without persons to assist at his grave but without a grave. Who will keep us then we know not; as long as we can, let us admit as much help as we can; another and another physician is not another and another indication and symptom of death, but another and another assistant, and proctor of life: nor do they so much feed the imagination with apprehension of danger, as the understanding with comfort. Let not one bring learning, another diligence, another religion, but every one bring all; and as many ingredients enter into a receipt, so may many men make the receipt. But why do I exercise my meditation so long upon this, of having plentiful help in time of need? Is not my meditation rather to be inclined another way, to condole and commiserate their distress who have none? How many are sicker (perchance) than I, and laid in their woful straw at home (if that corner be a home), and have no more hope of help, though they die, than of preferment, though they live! Nor do more expect to see a physician then, than to be an officer after; of whom, the first that takes knowledge, is the sexton that buries them, who buries them in oblivion too! For they do but fill up the number of the dead in the bill, but we shall never hear their names, till we read them in the book of life with our own. How many are sicker (perchance) than I, and thrown into hospitals, where (as a fish left upon the sand must stay the tide) they must stay the physician's hour of visiting, and then can be but visited! How many are sicker (perchance) than all we, and have not this hospital to cover them, not this straw to lie in, to die in, but have their gravestone under them, and breathe out their souls in the ears and in the eyes of passengers, harder than their bed, the flint of the street? that taste of no part of our physic, but a sparing diet, to whom ordinary porridge would be julep enough, the refuse of our servants bezoar enough, and the offscouring of our kitchen tables cordial enough. O my soul, when thou art not enough awake to bless thy God enough for his plentiful mercy in affording thee many helpers, remember how many lack them, and help them to them or to those other things which they lack as much as them.

VII.   EXPOSTULATION.

M Y God, my God, thy blessed servant Augustine begged of thee that Moses might come and tell him what he meant by some places of Genesis: may I have leave to ask of that Spirit that writ that book, why, when David expected news from Joab's army,[1] and that the watchman told him that he saw a man running alone, David concluded out of that circumstance, that if he came alone, he brought good news?[2]   I see the grammar, the word signifies so, and is so ever accepted, *good news;* but I see not the logic nor the rhetoric, how David would prove or persuade that his news was good because he was alone, except a greater company might have made great impressions of danger, by imploring and importuning present supplies.   Howsoever that be, I am sure that that which thy apostle says to Timothy, *Only Luke is with me,*[3] Luke, and nobody but Luke, hath a taste of complaint and sorrow in it: though Luke want no testimony of ability, of forwardness, of constancy, and perseverance, in assisting that great building which St. Paul laboured in, yet St. Paul is affected with that, that there was none but Luke to assist.   We take St. Luke to have been a physician, and it admits the application the better that in the presence of one good physician we may be glad of more.   It was not only a civil spirit of policy, or order, that moved Moses's father-in-law to persuade him to divide the burden of government and judicature with others, and take others to his assistance,[4] but it was also thy immediate Spirit, O my God, that moved Moses

---

[1] 2 Sam. xviii. 25.
[2] So all but our translation takes it; even Buxdor and Schindler.
[3] 2 Tim. iv. 11.   [4] Exod. xviii. 13.

to present unto thee seventy of the elders of Israel,[5] to receive of that Spirit, which was upon Moses only before, such a portion as might ease him in the government of that people; though Moses alone had endowments above all, thou gavest him other assistants. I consider thy plentiful goodness, O my God, in employing angels more than one in so many of thy remarkable works. Of thy Son, thou sayest, *Let all the angels of God worship him;*[6] if that be in heaven, upon earth he says, *that he could command twelve legions of angels;*[7] and when heaven and earth shall be all one, at the last day, thy Son, O God, *the Son of man, shall come in his glory, and all the holy angels with him.*[8] The angels that celebrated his birth to the shepherds,[9] the angels that celebrated his second birth, his resurrection, to the Maries,[10] were in the plural, angels associated with angels. In Jacob's ladder,[11] they who ascended and descended, and maintained the trade between heaven and earth, between thee and us, they who have the commission, and charge to guide us in all our ways,[12] they who hastened Lot,[13] and in him, us, from places of danger and temptation, they who are appointed to instruct and govern us in the church here,[14] they who are sent to punish the disobedient and refractory,[15] that they are to be mowers and harvestmen[16] after we are grown up in one field, the church, at the day of judgment, they that are to carry our souls whither they carried Lazarus,[17] they who attended at the several gates of the new Jerusalem,[18] to admit us there; all these who administer to thy servants, from the first to their last, are angels, angels in the plural, in every service angels associated with angels. The

.[5] Num. xi. 16.   .[6] Heb. i. 6.   .[7] Matt. xxvi. 53.
.[8] Matt. xxv. 31.   .[9] Luke, ii. 13, 14.   [10] John, xx. 12.
[11] Gen. xxviii. 12.   [12] Psalm xci. 11.   [13] Gen. xix. 15.
[14] Rev. i. 20.   [15] Rev. viii. 2.   [16] Matt. xiii. 39.
[17] Luke, xvi. 22.   [18] Rev. xxi. 12.

power of a single angel we see in that one, who in one night destroyed almost two hundred thousand in Sennacherib's army,[19] yet thou often employest many; as we know the power of salvation is abundantly in any one evangelist, and yet thou hast afforded us four. Thy Son proclaims of himself that *the Spirit hath anointed him to preach the Gospel,*[20] yet he hath given others *for the perfecting of the saints in the work of the ministry.*[21] Thou hast made him *Bishop of our souls,*[22] but there are others bishops too. He gave the Holy Ghost,[23] and others gave it also. Thy way, O my God (and, O my God, thou lovest to walk in thine own ways, for they are large), thy way from the beginning, is multiplication of thy helps; and therefore it were a degree of ingratitude not to accept this mercy of affording me many helps for my bodily health, as a type and earnest of thy gracious purpose now and ever to afford me the same assistances. That for thy great help, thy word, I may seek that not from comers nor conventicles nor schismatical singularities, but from the association and communion of thy Catholic church, and those persons whom thou hast always furnished that church withal: and that I may associate thy word with thy sacrament, thy seal with thy patent; and in that sacrament associate the sign with the thing signified, the bread with the body of thy Son, so as I may be sure to have received both, and to be made thereby (as thy blessed servant Augustine says) the ark, and the monument, and the tomb of thy most blessed Son, that he, and all the merits of his death, may, by that receiving, be buried in me, to my quickening in this world, and my immortal establishing in the next.

[19] 2 Kings, xix. 35. [20] Luke, iv. 18. [21] Eph. iv. 12.
[22] I Pet. ii. 25. [23] John, xx. 22.

VII. PRAYER.

O ETERNAL and most gracious God, who gavest to thy servants in the wilderness thy manna, bread so conditioned, qualified so, as that to every man manna tasted like that which that man liked best, I humbly beseech thee to make this correction, which I acknowledge to be part of my daily bread, to taste so to me, not as I would but as thou wouldst have it taste, and to conform my taste, and make it agreeable to thy will. Thou wouldst have thy corrections taste of humiliation, but thou wouldst have them taste of consolation too; taste of danger, but taste of assurance too. As therefore thou hast imprinted in all thine elements of which our bodies consist two manifest qualities, so that as thy fire dries, so it heats too; and as thy water moists, so it cools too; so, O Lord, in these corrections which are the elements of our regeneration, by which our souls are made thine, imprint thy two qualities, those two operations, that, as they scourge us, they may scourge us into the way to thee; that when they have showed us that we are nothing in ourselves, they may also show us, that thou art all things unto us. When therefore in this particular circumstance, O Lord (but none of thy judgments are circumstances, they are all of all substance of thy good purpose upon us), when in this particular, that he whom thou hast sent to assist me, desires assistants to him, thou hast let me see in how few hours thou canst throw me beyond the help of man, let me by the same light see that no vehemence of sickness, no temptation of Satan, no guiltiness of sin, no prison of death, not this first, this sick bed, not the other prison, the close and dark grave, can remove me from the determined and good purpose which thou hast sealed concerning me. Let me think no degree of this thy correction casual, or without signification; but yet when I have read it in that language, as a correction, let me translate it into another, and read it as a mercy; and which of these is the original, and which is the translation; whether thy mercy or thy correction were thy primary and original intention in this sickness, I cannot conclude, though death conclude me; for as it must necessarily appear to be a correction, so I can have no greater argument of thy mercy, than to die in thee and by that death to be united to him who died for me.

VIII. Et Rex ipse suum mittit.

The King sends his own physician.

VIII. MEDITATION.

STILL when we return to that meditation that man is a world, we find new discoveries. Let him be a world, and himself will be the land, and misery the sea. His misery (for misery is his, his own; of the happiness even of this world, he is but tenant, but of misery the freeholder; of happiness he is but the farmer, but the usufructuary, but of misery the lord, the proprietary), his misery, as the sea, swells above all the hills, and reaches to the remotest parts of this earth, man; who of himself is but dust, and coagulated and kneaded into earth by tears; his matter is earth, his form misery. In this world that is mankind, the highest ground, the eminentest hills, are kings; and have they line and lead enough to fathom this sea, and say, My misery is but this deep? Scarce any misery equal to sickness, and they are subject to that equally with their lowest subject. A glass is not the less brittle, because a king's face is represented in it; nor a king the less brittle, because God is represented in him. They have physicians continually about them, and therefore sickness, or the worst of sicknesses, continual fear of it. Are they gods? He that called them so cannot flatter. They are gods, but sick gods ; and God is presented to us under many human affections, as far as infirmities: God is called angry, and sorry, and weary, and heavy, but never a sick God; for then he might die like men, as our gods do. The worst that they could say in reproach and scorn of the gods of the heathen was, that perchance they were asleep; but gods that are so sick as that they cannot sleep are in an infirmer condition. A god, and need a physician? A Jupiter, and need an Æsculapius? that must have rhubarb to purge his choler lest he be too angry, and agarick to purge his phlegm lest he be too drowsy; that as Tertullian says of the Egyptian gods, plants and herbs, that " God was beholden to man for growing in his garden," so we must say of these gods, their eternity (an eternity of threescore and ten years) is in the apothecary's shop, and not in the metaphorical deity. But their deity is better expressed in their humility than in their height; when abounding and overflowing, as God, in means of doing good, they descend, as God, to a communication of their abundances with men according to their necessities, then they are gods. No man is well that understands not, that values not his being well; that hath not a cheerfulness and a joy in it; and whosoever hath this joy hath a desire to communicate, to propagate that which occasions his happiness and his joy to others; for every man loves witnesses of his happiness, and the best witnesses are experimental witnesses; they who have tasted of that in themselves which makes us happy. It consummates therefore, it perfects the happiness of kings,

to confer, to transfer, honour and riches, and (as they can)
health, upon those that need them.

VIII. EXPOSTULATION.

MY God, my God, I have a warning from the wise
man, that *when a rich man speaketh every man
holdeth his tongue, and, look, what he saith, they
extol it to the clouds; but if a poor man speak, they say,
What fellow is this? And if he stumble, they will help to
overthrow him.*[1] Therefore may my words be under-
valued and my errors aggravated, if I offer to speak of
kings; but not by thee, O my God, because I speak of
them as they are in thee, and of thee as thou art in them.
Certainly those men prepare a way of speaking negligently
or irreverently of thee, that give themselves that liberty
in speaking of thy vicegerents, kings; for thou who gavest
Augustus the empire, gavest it to Nero too; and as
Vespasian had it from thee, so had Julian. Though kings
deface in themselves thy first image in their own soul,
thou givest no man leave to deface thy second image,
imprinted indelibly in their power. But thou knowest,
O God, that if I should be slack in celebrating thy mercies
to me exhibited by that royal instrument, my sovereign,
to many other faults that touch upon allegiance I should
add the worst of all, ingratitude, which constitutes an ill
man; and faults which are defects in any particular
function are not so great as those that destroy our
humanity. It is not so ill to be an ill subject as to be an
ill man; for he hath an universal illness, ready to flow and
pour out itself into any mould, any form, and to spend
itself in any function. As therefore thy Son did upon

[1] Ecclus. xiii. 23.

52

the coin, I look upon the king, and I ask whose image and whose inscription he hath, and he hath thine; and I give unto thee that which is thine; I recommend his happiness to thee in all my sacrifices of thanks, for that which he enjoys, and in all my prayers for the continuance and enlargement of them.   But let me stop, my God, and consider; will not this look like a piece of art and cunning, to convey into the world an opinion that I were more particular in his care than other men? and that herein, in a show of humility and thankfulness, I magnify myself more than there is cause?   But let not that jealousy stop me, O God, but let me go forward in celebrating thy mercy exhibited by him.   This which he doth now, in assisting so my bodily health, I know is common to me with many: many, many have tasted of that expression of his graciousness.   Where he can give health by his own hands he doth, and to more than any of his predecessors have done: therefore hath God reserved one disease for him, that he only might cure it, though perchance not only by one title and interest, nor only as one king.   To those that need it not, in that kind, and so cannot have it by his own hand, he sends a donative of health in sending his physician.   The holy king St. Louis, in France, and our Maud, is celebrated for that, that personally they visited hospitals, and assisted in the cure even of loathsome diseases.   And when that religious Empress Placilla, the wife of Theodosius, was told that she diminished herself too much in those personal assistances and might do enough in sending relief, she said she would send in that capacity as a Christian, as a fellow-member of the body of thy Son, with them.   So thy servant David applies himself to his people, so he incorporates himself in his people, by calling them his brethren, his bones, his flesh;[2]

[2] 2 Sam. xix. 12.

and when they fell under thy hand, even to the preter-
mitting of himself, he presses upon thee by prayer for
them; *I have sinned, but these sheep, what have they done?*
Let thine hand, I pray thee, be against me and against my
father's house.[3] It is kingly to give; when Araunah gave
that great and free present to David, that place, those
instruments for sacrifice, and the sacrifices themselves, it
is said there by thy Spirit, *All these things did Araunah*
give, as a king, to the king.[4] To give is an approaching
to the condition of kings, but to give health, an approaching
to the King of kings, to thee.   But this his assisting to my
bodily health, thou knowest, O God, and so do some others
of thine honourable servants know, is but the twilight of
that day wherein thou, through him, hast shined upon
me before; but the echo of that voice, whereby thou,
through him, hast spoke to me before, then when
he, first of any man, conceived a hope that
I might be of some use in thy church and descended
to an intimation, to a persuasion, almost to a solicitation, that I would embrace that calling.   And thou
who hadst put that desire into his heart, didst also put
into mine an obedience to it; and I, who was sick before
of a vertiginous giddiness and irresolution, and almost
spent all my time in consulting how I should spend it,
was by this man of God, and God of men, put into the
pool and recovered: when I asked, perchance, a stone, he
gave me bread; when I asked, perchance, a scorpion, he
gave me a fish; when I asked a temporal office, he denied
not, refused not that; but let me see that he had rather I
took this.   These things thou, O God, who forgettest
nothing, hast not forgot, though perchance he, because
they were benefits, hath; but I am not only a witness, but
an instance, that our Jehoshaphat hath a care to ordain

[3] 2 Sam. xxiv. 17.   [4] 2 Sam. xxiv. 22, 23,

priests, as well as judges:[5] and not only to send physicians for temporal but to be the physician for spiritual health.

VIII. PRAYER.

O ETERNAL and most gracious God, who, though thou have reserved thy treasure of perfect joy and perfect glory to be given by thine own hands then, when, by seeing thee as thou art in thyself, and knowing thee as we are known, we shall possess in an instant, and possess for ever, all that can any way conduce to our happiness, yet here also, in this world, givest us such earnests of that full payment, as by the value of the earnest we may give some estimate of the treasure, humbly and thankfully I acknowledge, that thy blessed Spirit instructs me to make a difference of thy blessings in this world, by that difference of the instruments by which it hath pleased thee to derive them unto me. As we see thee here in a glass, so we receive from thee here by reflection and by instruments. Even casual things come from thee; and that which we call fortune here hath another name above. Nature reaches out her hand and gives us corn, and wine, and oil, and milk; but thou fillest her hand before, and thou openest her hand that she may rain down her showers upon us. Industry reaches out her hand to us and gives us fruits of our labour for ourselves and our posterity; but thy hand guides that hand when it sows and when it waters, and the increase is from thee. Friends reach out their hands and prefer us; but thy hand supports that hand that supports us. Of all these thy instruments have I received thy blessing, O God; but bless thy name most for the

[5] 2 Chron. xix. 8.

greatest; that, as a member of the public, and as a partaker of private favours too, by thy right hand, thy powerful hand set over us, I have had my portion not only in the hearing, but in the preaching of thy Gospel. Humbly beseeching thee, that as thou continuest thy wonted goodness upon the whole world by the wonted means and instruments, the same sun and moon, the same nature and industry, so to continue the same blessings upon this state and this church by the same hand, so long as that thy Son, when he comes in the clouds, may find him, or his son, or his son's sons ready to give an account and able to stand in that judgment, for their faithful stewardship and dispensation of thy talents so abundantly committed to them; and be to him, O God, in all distempers of his body, in all anxieties of spirit, in all holy sadnesses of soul, such a physician in thy proportion, who are the greatest in heaven, as he hath been in soul and body to me, in his proportion, who is the greatest upon earth.

IX.   MEDICAMINA SCRIBUNT.

Upon their consultation they prescribe.

IX.   MEDITATION.

THEY have seen me and heard me, arraigned me in these fetters and received the evidence ; I have cut up mine own anatomy, dissected myself, and they are gone to read upon me.   O how manifold and perplexed a thing, nay, how wanton and various a thing, is ruin and destruction!   God presented to David three kinds, war, famine and pestilence; Satan left out these, and brought in fires from heaven and winds from the wilderness.   If there were no ruin but sickness, we see the masters of that art can scarce number, not name all sicknesses; every thing that disorders a faculty, and the function of that, is a sickness; the names will not serve them which are given from the place affected, the pleurisy is so; nor from the effect which it works, the falling sickness is so; they cannot have names enough, from what it does, nor where it is, but they must extort names from what it is like, what it resembles, and but in some one thing, or else they would lack names; for the wolf, and the canker, and the polypus are so; and that question whether there be more names or things, is as perplexed in sicknesses as in any thing else; except it be easily resolved upon that side that there are more sicknesses than names. If ruin were reduced to that one way, that man could perish no way but by sickness, yet his danger were infinite; and if sickness were reduced to that one way, that there were no sickness but a fever, yet the way were infinite still; for it would overload and oppress any natural, disorder and discompose any artificial, memory, to deliver the names of several fevers; how intricate a work then have they who are gone to consult which of these sicknesses mine is, and then which of these fevers, and then what it would do, and then how it may be countermined. But even in ill it is a degree of good when the evil will admit consultation. In many diseases, that which is but an accident, but a symptom of the main disease, is so violent, that the physician must attend the cure of that, though he pretermit (so far as to intermit) the cure of the disease itself. Is it not so in states too? Sometimes the insolency of those that are great puts the people into commotions; the great disease, and the greatest danger to the head, is the insolency of the great ones; and yet they execute martial law, they come to present executions upon the people, whose commotion was indeed but a symptom, but an accident of the main disease; but this symptom, grown so violent, would allow no time for a consultation. Is it not so in the accidents of the diseases of our mind too? Is it not evidently so in our affections, in our passions? If a choleric n.an be ready to strike, must I go about to purge his choler, or to break the blow? But where there is room for consultation things are not desperate. They consult, so there is nothing rashly, inconsiderately done; and then they prescribe, they write, so there is nothing covertly, disguisedly, unavowedly done. In bodily diseases it is not always so; sometimes, as soon as the physician's foot is in the chamber, his knife is in the patient's arm; the disease would not allow a minute's forbearing of blood, nor prescribing of other remedies. In states and matter of government it is so too; they are sometimes surprised with such accidents, as that the magistrate asks not what may be done by law, but does that which must necessarily be done in that case. But it is a degree of good in evil, a degree that carries hope and comfort in it, when we may have recourse to that which is written, and that the proceedings may be apert, and ingenuous, and candid, and avowable, for that gives satisfaction and acquiescence. They who have received my anatomy of myself consult, and end their consultation in prescribing, and in prescribing physic; proper and convenient remedy; for if they should come in again and chide me for some disorder that had occasioned and induced, or that had hastened and exalted this sickness, or if they should begin to write now rules for my diet and exercise when I were well, this were to antedate or to postdate their consultation, not to give physic. It were rather a vexation than a relief, to tell a condemned prisoner, You might have lived if you had done this; and if you can get your pardon, you shall do well to take this or this course hereafter. I am glad they know (I have hid nothing from them), glad they consult (they hid nothing from one another), glad they write (they hide nothing from the world), glad that they write and prescribe physic, that there are remedies for the present case.

IX. EXPOSTULATION.

MY God, my God, allow me a just indignation, a holy detestation of the insolency of that man who, because he was of that high rank, of whom thou hast said, *They are gods,* thought himself more than equal to thee; that king of Aragon, Alphonsus, so perfect in the motions of the heavenly bodies as that he adventured to say, that if he had been of counsel with thee, in the making of the heavens, the heavens should have been disposed in a better order than they are. The king Amaziah would not endure thy prophet to reprehend him, but asked him in anger, *Art thou made of the king's counsel?*[1] When thy prophet Esaias asks that question, *Who hath directed the spirit of the Lord, or being his counsellor, hath taught him?*[2] it is after he had settled and determined that office upon thy Son, and him only, when he joins with those great titles, the mighty God and the Prince of peace, this also, the Counsellor;[3] and after he had settled upon him the spirit of might and of counsel.[4] So that then thou, O God, though thou have no counsel from man, yet dost nothing upon man without counsel. In the making of man there was a consultation; *Let us make man.*[5] In the preserving of man, *O thou great Preserver of men,*[6] thou proceedest by counsel; for all thy

[1] 2 Chron. xxv. 16. 2 Isaiah, xlii. 13. [3] Isaiah, ix. 6.
[4] Isaiah, xi. 2. [5] Gen. i. 26. [6] Job, vii. 20.

external works are the works of the whole Trinity, and their hand is to every action. How much more must I apprehend that all you blessed and glorious persons of the Trinity are in consultation now, what you will do with this infirm body, with this leprous soul, that attends guiltily, but yet comfortably, your determination upon it. I offer not to counsel them who meet in consultation for my body now, but I open my infirmities, I anatomize my body to them. So I do my soul to thee, O my God, in an humble confession, that there is no vein in me that is not full of the blood of thy Son, whom I have crucified and crucified again, by multiplying many, and often repeating the same, sins; that there is no artery in me that hath not the spirit of error, the spirit of lust, the spirit of giddiness in it;[7] no bone in me that is not hardened with the custom of sin and nourished and suppled with the marrow of sin; no sinews, no ligaments, that do not tie and chain sin and sin together. Yet, O blessed and glorious Trinity, O holy and whole college, and yet but one physician, if you take this confession into a consultation, my case is not desperate, my destruction is not decreed. If your consultation determine in writing, if you refer me to that which is written, you intend my recovery: for all the way, O my God (ever constant to thine own ways), thou hast proceeded openly, intelligibly, manifestly by the book. From thy first book, the book of life, never shut to thee, but never thoroughly open to us; from thy second book, the book of nature, where, though subobscurely and in shadows, thou hast expressed thine own image; from thy third book, the Scriptures, where thou hadst written all in the Old, and then lightedst us a candle to read it by, in the New, Testament; to these thou hadst added the book of just

[7] I Tim. iv. I; Hos. iv. 12; Isaiah, xix. 14.

and useful laws, established by them to whom thou hast committed thy people; to those, the manuals, the pocket, the bosom books of our own consciences; to those thy particular books of all our particular sins; and to those, the books with seven seals, which only *the Lamb which was slain, was found worthy to open;*[8] which, I hope, it shall not disagree with the meaning of thy blessed Spirit to interpret the promulgation of their pardon and righteousness who are washed in the blood of that Lamb; and if thou refer me to these books, to a new reading, a new trial by these books, this fever may be but a burning in the hand and I may be saved, though not by my book, mine own conscience, nor by thy other books, yet by thy first, the book of life, thy decree for my election, and by thy last, the book of the Lamb, and the shedding of his blood upon me. If I be still under consultation, I am not condemned yet; if I be sent to these books, I shall not be condemned at all; for though there be something written in some of those books (particularly in the Scriptures) which some men turn to poison, yet upon these consultations (these confessions, these takings of our particular cases into thy consideration) thou intendest all for physic; and even from those sentences from which a too late repenter will suck desperation, he that seeks thee early shall receive thy morning dew, thy seasonable mercy, thy forward consolation.

IX. PRAYER.

O ETERNAL and most gracious God, who art of so pure eyes as that thou canst not look upon sin, and we of so unpure constitutions as that we can present no object but sin, and therefore might justly fear

[8] Rev. vii. 1.

that thou wouldst turn thine eyes for ever from us, as, though we cannot endure afflictions in ourselves, yet in thee we can; so, though thou canst not endure sin in us, yet in thy Son thou canst, and he hath taken upon himself, and presented to thee, all those sins which might displease thee in us. There is an eye in nature that kills as soon as it sees, the eye of a serpent; no eye in nature that nourishes us by looking upon us; but thine eye, O Lord, does so. Look therefore upon me, O Lord, in this distress and that will recall me from the borders of this bodily death; look upon me, and that will raise me again from that spiritual death in which my parents buried me when they begot me in sin, and in which I have pierced even to the jaws of hell by multiplying such heaps of actual sins upon that foundation, that root of original sin. Yet take me again into your consultation, O blessed and glorious Trinity; and though the Father know that I have defaced his image received in my creation; though the Son know I have neglected mine interest in the redemption; yet, O blessed Spirit, as thou art to my conscience so be to them, a witness that, at this minute, I accept that which I have so often, so rebelliously refused, thy blessed inspirations; be thou my witness to them that, at more pores than this slack body sweats tears, this sad soul weeps blood; and more for the displeasure of my God, than for the stripes of his displeasure. Take me, then, O blessed and glorious Trinity, into a reconsultation, and prescribe me any physic. If it be a long and painful holding of this soul in sickness, it is physic if I may discern thy hand to give it; and it is physic if it be a speedy departing of this soul, if I may discern thy hand to receive it.

X. Lente et serpenti satagunt occurrere morbo.

*They find the disease to steal on insensibly, and endeavour
to meet with it so.*

X. MEDITATION.

THIS is nature's nest of boxes: the heavens contain the earth; the earth, cities; cities, men.   And all these are concentric; the common centre to them all is decay, ruin; only that is eccentric which was never made; only that place, or garment rather, which we can imagine but not demonstrate.   That light, which is the very emanation of the light of God, in which the saints shall dwell, with which the saints shall be apparelled, only that bends not to this centre, to ruin; that which was not made of nothing is not threatened with this annihilation. All other things are; even angels, even our souls; they move upon the same poles, they bend to the same centre; and if they were not made immortal by preservation, their nature could not keep them from sinking to this centre, annihilation.   In all these (the frame of the heavens, the states upon earth, and men in them, comprehend all), those are the greatest mischiefs which are least discerned; the most insensible in their ways come to be the most sensible in their ends.   The heavens have had their dropsy, they drowned the world; and they shall have their fever, and burn the world.   Of the dropsy, the flood, the world had a foreknowledge one hundred and twenty years before it came; and so some made provision against it, and were saved; the fever shall break out in an instant and consume all; the dropsy did no harm to the heavens from whence it fell, it did not put out those lights, it did not quench those heats; but the fever, the fire, shall burn the furnace itself, annihilate those heavens that breathe it out. Though the dogstar have a pestilent breath, an infectious exhalation, yet, because we know when it will rise, we clothe ourselves, and we diet ourselves, and we shadow ourselves to a sufficient prevention; but comets and blazing stars, whose effects or significations no man can interrupt or frustrate, no man foresaw: no almanack tells us when a blazing star will break out, the matter is carried up in secret; no astrologer tells us when the effects will be accomplished, for that is a secret of a higher sphere than the other; and that which is most secret is most dangerous. It is so also here in the societies of men, in states and commonwealths. Twenty rebellious drums make not so dangerous a noise as a few whisperers and secret plotters in corners. The cannon doth not so much hurt against a wall, as a mine under the wall; nor a thousand enemies that threaten, so much as a few that take an oath to say nothing. God knew many heavy sins of the people, in the wilderness and after, but still he charges them with that one, with murmuring, murmuring in their hearts, secret disobediences, secret repugnances against his declared will; and these are the most deadly, the most pernicious. And it is so too with the diseases of the body; and that is my case. The pulse, the urine, the sweat, all have sworn to say nothing, to give no indication of any dangerous sickness. My forces are not enfeebled, I find no decay in my strength; my provisions are not cut off, I find no abhorring in mine appetite; my counsels are not corrupted nor infatuated, I find no false apprehensions to work upon mine understanding; and yet they see that invisibly, and I feel that insensibly, the disease prevails. The disease hath established a kingdom, an empire in me, and will have certain *arcana imperii*, secrets of state, by which it will proceed and not be bound to declare them. But yet against those secret conspiracies in the state, the magistrate hath the rack; and against these insensible diseases physicians have their examiners; and those these employ now.

X. EXPOSTULATION.

MY God, my God, I have been told, and told by relation, by her own brother that did it, by thy servant Nazianzen, that his sister in the vehemency of her prayer, did use to threaten thee with a holy importunity, with a pious impudency. I dare not do so, O God; but as thy servant Augustine wished that Adam had not sinned, therefore that Christ might not have died, may I not to this one purpose wish that if the serpent, before the temptation of Eve, did go upright and speak,[1] that he did so still, because I should the sooner hear him if he spoke, the sooner see him if he went upright? In his curse I am cursed too; his creeping undoes me; for howsoever he begin at the heel, and do but bruise that, yet he, and *death* in him, *is come into our windows*;[2] into our eyes and ears, the entrances and inlets of our soul. He works upon us in secret and we do not discern him; and one great work of his upon us is to make us so like himself as to sin in secret, that others may not see us; but his masterpiece is to make us sin in secret, so as that we may not see ourselves sin. For the first, the hiding of our sins from other men, he hath induced that which was his offspring from the beginning, a lie;[3] for man is, in nature, yet in possession of some such sparks of ingenuity and nobleness, as that, but to disguise evil,

[1] Josephus. [2] Jer. ix. 21. [3] John, viii. 44.

he would not lie. The body, the sin, is the serpent's; and the garment that covers it, the lie, is his too. These are his, but the hiding of sin from ourselves is he himself: when we have the sting of the serpent in us, and do not sting ourselves, the venom of sin, and no remorse for sin, then, as thy blessed Son said of Judas, *He is a devil;*[4] not that he had one, but was one; so we are become devils to ourselves, and we have not only a serpent in our bosom, but we ourselves are to ourselves that serpent. How far did thy servant David press upon thy pardon in that petition, *Cleanse thou me from secret sins?*[5] Can any sin be secret? for a great part of our sins, though, says thy prophet, we conceive them in the dark, upon our bed, yet, says he, we do them in the light; there are many sins which we glory in doing, and would not do if nobody should know them. Thy blessed servant Augustine confesses that he was ashamed of his shamefacedness and tenderness of conscience, and that he often belied himself with sins which he never did, lest he should be unacceptable to his sinful companions. But if we would conceal them (thy prophet found such a desire, and such a practice in some, when he said, *Thou hast trusted in thy wickedness, and thou hast said, None shall see me*[6]), yet can we conceal them? Thou, O God, canst hear of them by others: the voice of Abel's blood will tell thee of Cain's murder;[7] the heavens themselves will tell thee. Heaven shall reveal his iniquity; a small creature alone shall do it, *A bird of the air shall carry the voice, and tell the matter;*[8] thou wilt trouble no informer, thou thyself revealedst Adam's sin to thyself;[9] and the manifestation of sin is so full to thee, as that thou shalt reveal all to all; *Thou shalt*

---

[4] John, vi. 70.　　　　　[5] Psalm xix. 12.
[6] Isaiah xlvii. 10.　　　[7] Gen. iv. 10.
[8] Eccles. x. 20.　　　　[9] Gen. iii. 8.

bring every work to judgment, with every secret thing;[10]
and there is nothing covered that shall not be revealed.[11]
But, O my God, there is another way of knowing my
sins, which thou lovest better than any of these; to know
them by my confession. As physic works, so it draws
the peccant humour to itself, that, when it is gathered
together, the weight of itself may carry that humour
away; so thy Spirit returns to my memory my former
sins, that, being so recollected, they may pour out themselves by confession. *When I kept silence,* says thy
servant David, *day and night thy hand was heavy upon
me;* but when I said, *I will confess my transgressions unto
the Lord, thou forgavest the iniquity of my sin.*[12] Thou
interpretest the very purpose of confession so well, as
that thou scarce leavest any new mercy for the action
itself. This mercy thou leavest, that thou armest us
thereupon against relapses into the sins which we have
confessed. And that mercy which thy servant Augustine
apprehends when he says to thee, " Thou hast forgiven
me those sins which I have done, and those sins
which only by thy grace I have not done ": they were
done in our inclination to them, and even that inclination
needs thy mercy, and that mercy he calls a pardon. And
these are most truly secret sins, because they were never
done, and because no other man, nor I myself, but only
thou knowest, how many and how great sins I have
escaped by thy grace, which, without that, I should have
multiplied against thee.

[10] Eccles. xii. 14.   [11] Matt. x. 26.   [12] Psalm xxxii. 3—5.

X. PRAYER.

O ETERNAL and most gracious God, who as thy Son Christ Jesus, though he knew all things, yet said he knew not the day of judgment, because he knew it not so as that he might tell us; so though thou knowest all my sins, yet thou knowest them not to my comfort, except thou know them by my telling them to thee. How shall I bring to thy knowledge, by that way, those sins which I myself know not? If I accuse myself of original sin, wilt thou ask me if I know what original sin is? I know not enough of it to satisfy others, but I know enough to condemn myself, and to solicit thee. If I confess to thee the sins of my youth, wilt thou ask me if I know what those sins were? I know them not so well as to name them all, nor am sure to live hours enough to name them all (for I did them then faster than I can speak them now, when every thing that I did conduced to some sin), but I know them so well as to know that nothing but thy mercy is so infinite as they. If the naming of sins of thought, word and deed, of sins of omission and of action, of sins against thee, against my neighbour and against myself, of sins unrepented and sins relapsed into after repentance, of sins of ignorance and sins against the testimony of my conscience, of sins against thy commandments, sins against thy Son's Prayer, and sins against our own creed, of sins against the laws of that church, and sins against the laws of that state in which thou hast given me my station; if the naming of these sins reach not home to all mine, I know what will. O Lord, pardon me, me, all those sins which thy Son Christ Jesus suffered for, who suffered for all the sins of all the world; for there is no sin amongst all those which had not been my sin, if thou hadst not been my God, and antedated me a pardon in thy preventing grace. And since sin, in the nature of it, retains still so much of the author of it that it is a serpent, insensibly insinuating itself into my soul, let thy brazen serpent (the contemplation of thy Son crucified for me) be evermore present to me, for my recovery against the sting of the first serpent; that so, as I have a Lion against a lion, the Lion of the tribe of Judah against that lion that seeks whom he may devour, so I may have a serpent against a serpent, the wisdom of the serpent against the malice of the serpent, and both against that lion and serpent, forcible and subtle temptations, thy dove with thy olive in thy ark, humility and peace and reconciliation to thee, by the ordinances of thy church. Amen.

XI. Nobilibusque trahunt, a cincto corde, venenum,
Succis et gemmis, et quæ generosa, ministrant
Ars, et natura, instillant.

They use cordials, to keep the venom and malignity of the disease from the heart.

XI. MEDITATION.

WHENCE can we take a better argument, a clearer demonstration, that all the greatness of this world is built upon opinion of others and hath in itself no real being, nor power of subsistence, than from the heart of man? It is always in action and motion, still busy, still pretending to do all, to furnish all the powers and faculties with all that they have; but if an enemy dare rise up against it, it is the soonest endangered, the soonest defeated of any part. The brain will hold out longer than it, and the liver longer than that; they will endure a siege; but an unnatural heat, a rebellious heat, will blow up the heart, like a mine, in a minute. But howsoever, since the heart hath the birthright and primogeniture, and that it is nature's eldest son in us, the part which is first born to life in man, and that the other parts, as younger brethren, and servants in his family, have a dependance upon it, it is reason that the principal care be had of it, though it be not the strongest part, as the eldest is oftentimes not the strongest of the family. And since the brain, and liver, and heart hold not a triumvirate in man, a sovereignty equally shed upon them all, for his well-being, as the four elements do for his very being, but the heart alone is in the principality, and in the throne, as king, the rest as subjects, though in eminent place and office, must contribute to that, as children to their parents, as all persons to all kinds of superiors, though oftentimes those parents or those superiors be not of stronger parts than themselves, that serve and obey them that are weaker. Neither doth this obligation fall upon us, by second dictates of nature, by consequences and conclusions arising out of nature, or derived from nature by discourse (as many things bind us even by the law of nature, and yet not by the primary law of nature; as all laws of propriety in that which we possess are of the law of nature, which law is, to give every one his own, and yet in the primary law of nature there was no propriety, no *meum et tuum*, but an universal community over all; so the obedience of superiors is of the law of nature, and yet in the primary law of nature there was no superiority, no magistracy); but this contribution of assistance of all to the sovereign, of all parts to the heart, is from the very first dictates of nature, which is, in the first place, to have care of our own preservation, to look first to ourselves; for therefore doth the physician intermit the present care of brain or liver, because there is a possibility that they may subsist, though there be not a present and a particular care had of them, but there is no possibility that they can subsist, if the heart perish: and so, when we seem to begin with others, in such assistances, indeed, we do begin with ourselves, and we ourselves are principally in our contemplation; and so all these officious and mutual assistances are but compliments towards others, and our true end is ourselves. And this is the reward of the pains of kings; sometimes they need the power of law to be obeyed; and when they seem to be obeyed voluntarily, they who do it do it for their own sakes. O how little a thing is all the greatness of man and through how false glasses doth he make shift to multiply it, and magnify it to himself! And yet this is also another misery of this king of man, the heart, which is also applicable to the kings of this world, great men, that the venom and poison of every pestilential disease directs itself to the heart, affects that (pernicious affection), and the malignity of ill men is also directed upon the greatest and the best; and not only greatness but goodness loses the vigour of being an antidote or cordial against it. And as the noblest and most generous cordials that nature or art afford, or can prepare, if they be often taken and made familiar, become no cordials, nor have any extraordinary operation, so the greatest cordial of the heart, patience, if it be much exercised, exalts the venom and the malignity of the enemy, and the more we suffer the more we are insulted upon. When God had made this earth of nothing, it was but a little help that he had, to make other things of this earth: nothing can be nearer nothing than this earth; and yet how little of this earth is the greatest man! He thinks he treads upon the earth, that all is under his feet, and the brain that thinks so is but earth; his highest region, the flesh that covers that, is but earth, and even the top of that, that wherein so many Absaloms take so much pride, is but a bush growing upon that turf of earth. How little of the world is the earth! And yet that is all that man hath or is. How little of a man is the heart, and yet it is all by which he is; and this continually subject not only to foreign poisons conveyed by others, but to intestine poisons bred in ourselves by pestilential sicknesses. O who, if before he had a being he could have sense of this misery, would buy a being here upon these conditions?

XI. EXPOSTULATION.

MY God, my God, all that thou askest of me is my heart, *My Son, give me thy heart.*[1] Am I thy Son as long as I have but my heart? Wilt thou give me an inheritance, a filiation, any thing for my heart? O thou, who saidst to Satan, *Hast thou considered my servant Job, that there is none like him upon the earth,*[2] shall my fear, shall my zeal, shall my jealousy, have leave to say to thee, Hast thou considered my heart, that there is not so perverse a heart upon earth; and wouldst thou have that, and shall I be thy son, thy eternal Son's coheir, for giving that? *The heart is deceitful above all things, and desperately wicked; who can know it?*[3] He that asks that question makes the answer, I the Lord search the heart. When didst thou search mine? Dost thou think to find it, as thou madest it, in Adam? Thou hast searched since, and found all these gradations in the ill of our hearts, *that every imagina-*

---

[1] Prov. xxiii. 26.   [2] Job, i. 8.   [3] Jer. xvii. 9.

72

tion of the thoughts of our hearts is only evil continually.[4]
Dost thou remember this, and wouldst thou have my
heart? O God of all light, I know thou knowest all,
and it is thou[5] that declarest unto man what is his heart.
Without thee, O sovereign Goodness, I could not know
how ill my heart were. Thou hast declared unto me, in
thy word, that for all this deluge of evil that hath surrounded all hearts, yet thou soughtest and foundest a man
after thine own heart;[6] that thou couldst and wouldst
give thy people pastors according to thine own heart;[7] and
I can gather out of thy word so good testimony of the
hearts of men as to find single hearts, docile and appre-
hensive hearts; hearts that can, hearts that have learned;
wise hearts in one place, and in another in a great degree
wise, perfect hearts; straight hearts, no perverseness
without; and clean hearts, no foulness within: such hearts
I can find in thy word; and if my heart were such a
heart, I would give thee my heart. But I find stony
hearts too,[8] and I have made mine such: I have found
hearts that are snares;[9] and I have conversed with such;
hearts that burn like ovens;[10] and the fuel of lust, and
envy, and ambition, hath inflamed mine; hearts in which
their masters trust, and *he that trusteth in his own heart is
a fool;*[11] his confidence in his own moral constancy and
civil fortitude will betray him, when thou shalt cast a
spiritual damp, a heaviness and dejection of spirit upon
him. I have found these hearts, and a worse than these,
a heart into the which the devil himself is entered, Judas's
heart.[12] The first kind of heart, alas, my God, I have
not; the last are not hearts to be given to thee. What
shall I do? Without that present I cannot be thy son,

[4] Gen. vi. 5.   [5] Amos, iv. 13.   [6] 1 Sam. xiii. 14.
[7] Jer. iii. 15.   [8] Ezek. xi. 19.   [9] Eccles. vii. 26.
[10] Hos. vii. 6.   [11] Prov. xxviii. 26.   [12] John, xiii. 2.

and I have it not. To those of the first kind thou givest joyfulness of heart,[13] and I have not that ; to those of the other kind thou givest faintness of heart ;[14] and blessed be thou, O God, for that forbearance, I have not that yet. There is then a middle kind of hearts, not so perfect as to be given but that the very giving mends them ; not so desperate as not to be accepted but that the very accepting dignifies them. This is a melting heart,[15] and a troubled heart, and a wounded heart, and a broken heart, and a contrite heart ; and by the powerful working of thy piercing Spirit such a heart I have. Thy Samuel spake unto all the house of thy Israel, and said, *If you return to the Lord with all your hearts, prepare your hearts unto the Lord.*[16] If my heart be prepared, it is a returning heart. And if thou see it upon the way, thou wilt carry it home. Nay, the preparation is thine too ; this melting, this wounding, this breaking, this contrition, which I have now, is thy way to thy end ; and those discomforts are, for all that, *the earnest of thy Spirit in my heart*;[17] and where thou givest earnest, thou wilt perform the bargain. Nabal was confident upon his wine, but *in the morning his heart died within him.*[18] Thou, O Lord, hast given me wormwood, and I have had some diffidence upon that ; and thou hast cleared a morning to me again, and my heart is alive. David's heart smote him when he cut off the skirt from Saul ;[19] and his heart smote him when he had numbered his people :[20] my heart hath struck me when I come to number my sins ; but that blow is not to death, because those sins are not to death, but my heart lives in thee. But yet as long as I remain in this great hospital, this sick, this diseaseful world, as long as I

---

13 Ecclus. l. 23.
15 Josh. ii. 11.
17 2 Cor. i. 22.
19 1 Sam. xxiv. 5.

14 Lev. xxvi. 36.
16 1 Sam. vii. 3.
18 1 Sam. xxv. 37.
20 2 Sam. xxiv. 10.

remain in this leprous house, this flesh of mine, this heart, though thus prepared for thee, prepared by thee, will still be subject to the invasion of malign and pestilent vapours. But I have my cordials in thy promise; *when I shall know the plague of my heart, and pray unto thee in thy house*,[21] thou wilt preserve that heart from all mortal force of that infection; *and the peace of God, which passeth all understanding, shall keep my heart and mind through Christ Jesus.*[22]

XI. PRAYER.

O ETERNAL and most gracious God, who in thy upper house, the heavens, though there be many mansions, yet art alike and equally in every mansion; but here in thy lower house, though thou fillest all, yet art otherwise in some rooms thereof than in others; otherwise in thy church than in my chamber, and otherwise in thy sacraments than in my prayers; so though thou be always present and always working in every room of this thy house, my body, yet I humbly beseech thee to manifest always a more effectual presence in my heart than in the other offices. Into the house of thine anointed, disloyal persons, traitors, will come; into thy house, the church, hypocrites and idolators will come; into some rooms of this thy house, my body, temptations will come, infections will come; but be my heart thy bedchamber, O my God, and thither let them not enter. Job made a covenant with his eyes, but not his making of that covenant, but thy dwelling in his heart, enabled him to keep that covenant. Thy Son himself had a sadness in his soul to death, and he had a reluctation, a deprecation of death, in the approaches thereof; but he had his cordial

[21] 1 Kings, viii. 38. [22] Phil. iv. 7.

too, *Yet not my will, but thine be done.* And as thou hast not delivered us, thine adopted sons, from these infectious temptations, so neither hast thou delivered us over to them, nor withheld thy cordials from us. I was baptized in thy cordial water against original sin, and I have drunk of thy cordial blood, for my recovery from actual and habitual sin, in the other sacrament. Thou, O Lord, who hast imprinted all medicinal virtues which are in all creatures, and hast made even the flesh of vipers to assist in cordials, art able to make this present sickness, everlasting health, this weakness, everlasting strength, and this very dejection and faintness of heart, a powerful cordial. When thy blessed Son cried out to thee, *My God, my God, why hast thou forsaken me?* thou didst reach out thy hand to him; but not to deliver his sad soul, but to receive his holy soul: neither did he longer desire to hold it of thee, but to recommend it to thee. I see thine hand upon me now, O Lord, and I ask not why it comes, what it intends; whether thou wilt bid it stay still in this body for some time, or bid it meet thee this day in paradise, I ask not, not in a wish, not in a thought. Infirmity of nature, curiosity of mind, are temptations that offer; but a silent and absolute obedience to thy will, even before I know it, is my cordial. Preserve that to me, O my God, and that will preserve me to thee; that, when thou hast catechised me with affliction here, I may take a greater degree, and serve thee in a higher place, in thy kingdom of joy and glory. Amen.

XII. ——————————— Spirante columba
Supposita pedibus, revocantur ad ima vapores.

They apply pigeons, to draw the vapours from the head.

XII. MEDITATION.

WHAT will not kill a man if a vapour will? How great an elephant, how small a mouse destroys! To die by a bullet is the soldier's daily bread; but few men die by hail-shot. A man is more worth than to be sold for single money; a life to be valued above a trifle. If this were a violent shaking of the air by thunder or by cannon, in that case the air is condensed above the thickness of water, of water baked into ice, almost petrified, almost made stone, and no wonder that kills; but that which is but a vapour, and a vapour not forced but breathed, should kill, that our nurse should overlay us, and air that nourishes us should destroy us, but that it is a half atheism to murmur against Nature, who is God's immediate commissioner, who would not think himself miserable to be put into the hands of Nature, who does not only set him up for a mark for others to shoot at, but delights herself to blow him up like a glass, till she see him break, even with her own breath? Nay, if this infectious vapour were sought for, or travelled to, as Pliny hunted after the vapour of Ætna and dared and challenged Death in the form of a vapour to do his worst, and felt the worst, he died; or if this vapour were met withal in an ambush, and we surprised with it, out of a long shut well, or out of a new opened mine, who would lament, who would accuse, when we had nothing to accuse, none to lament against but fortune, who is less than a vapour? But when ourselves are the well that

77

breathes out this exhalation, the oven that spits out this fiery smoke, the mine that spews out this suffocating and strangling damp, who can ever, after this, aggravate his sorrow by this circumstance, that it was his neighbour, his familiar friend, his brother, that destroyed him, and destroyed him with a whispering and a calumniating breath, when we ourselves do it to ourselves by the same means, kill ourselves with our own vapours? Or if these occasions of this self-destruction had any contribution from our own wills, any assistance from our own intentions, nay, from our own errors, we might divide the rebuke, and chide ourselves as much as them. Fevers upon wilful distempers of drink and surfeits, consumptions upon intemperances and licentiousness, madness upon misplacing or overbending our natural faculties, proceed from ourselves, and so as that ourselves are in the plot, and we are not only passive, but active too, to our own destruction. But what have I done, either to breed or to breathe these vapours? They tell me it is my melancholy; did I infuse, did I drink in melancholy into myself? It is my thoughtfulness; was I not made to think? It is my study; doth not my calling call for that? I have done nothing wilfully, perversely toward it, yet must suffer in it, die by it. There are too many examples of men that have been their own executioners, and that have made hard shift to be so: some have always had poison about them, in a hollow ring upon their finger, and some in their pen that they used to write with; some have beat out their brains at the wall of their prison, and some have eat the fire out of their chimneys;[1] and one is said to have come nearer our case than so, to have strangled himself, though his hands were bound, by crushing his throat between his knees. But I do nothing

[1] Coma, latro. in Val. Max.

78

upon myself, and yet am mine own executioner. And we have heard of death upon small occasions and by scornful instruments: a pin, a comb, a hair pulled, hath gangrened and killed; but when I have said a vapour, if I were asked again what is a vapour, I could not tell, it is so insensible a thing; so near nothing is that that reduces us to nothing. But extend this vapour, rarefy it; from so narrow a room as our natural bodies, to any politic body, to a state. That which is fume in us is, in a state rumour; and these vapours in us, which we consider here pestilent and infectious fumes, are, in a state, infecitious rumours, detracting and dishonourable calumnies, libels, The heart in that body is the king, and the bran his council; and the whole magistracy, that ties all together, is the sinews which proceed from thence; and the life of all is honour, and just respect, and due reverence; and therefore, when these vapours, these venomous rumours, are directed against these noble parts, the whole body suffers. But yet for all their privileges, they are not privileged from our misery; that as the vapours most pernicious to us arise in our own bodies, so do the most dishonourable rumours, and those that wound a state most arise at home. What ill air that I could have met in the street, what channel, what shambles, what dunghill, what vault, could have hurt me so much as these home-bred vapours? What fugitive, what almsman of any foreign state, can do so much harm as a detractor, a libeller, a scornful jester at home? For as they that write of poisons, and of creatures naturally disposed to the ruin of man, do as well mention the flea as the viper[2], because the flea, though he kill none, he does all the harm he can; so even these libellous and licentious jesters utter the venom they have, though sometimes virtue, and always

[2] Ardoinus.

79

power, be a good pigeon to draw this vapour from the head and from doing any deadly harm there.

XII. EXPOSTULATION.

MY God, my God, as thy servant James, when he asks that question, *What is your life?* provides me my answer, *It is even a vapour, that appeareth for a little time, and then vanisheth away;*[3] so, if he did ask me what is your death, I am provided of my answer, it is a vapour too; and why should it not be all one to me, whether I live or die, if life and death be all one, both a vapour? Thou hast made vapour so indifferent a thing as that thy blessings and thy judgments are equally expressed by it, and is made by thee the hieroglyphic of both. Why should not that be always good by which thou hast declared thy plentiful goodness to us? *A vapour went up from the earth, and watered the whole face of the ground.*[4] And that by which thou hast imputed a goodness to us, and wherein thou hast accepted our service to thee, sacrifices; for sacrifices were vapours;[5] and in them it is said, that a *thick cloud of incense went up to thee.*[6] So it is of that wherein thou comest to us, the dew of heaven, and of that wherein we come to thee, both are vapours; and he, in whom we have and are all that we are or have, temporally or spiritually, thy blessed Son, in the person of Wisdom, is called so too; *She is* (that is, he is) *the vapour of the power of God, and the pure influence from the glory of the Almighty.*[7] Hast thou, thou, O my God, perfumed vapour with thine own breath, with so many sweet acceptations in thine own word, and shall this

---

[3] James, iv. 14.   [4] Gen. ii. 6.   [5] Lev. xvi. 13.
[6] Ezek. viii. 11.   [7] Wisd. vii. 25.

vapour receive an ill and infectious sense? It must; for, since we have displeased thee with that which is but vapour (for what is sin but a vapour, but a smoke, though such a smoke as takes away our sight, and disables us from seeing our danger), it is just that thou punish us with vapours too. For so thou dost, as the wise man tells us, thou canst punish us by those things wherein we offend thee; as he hath expressed it there, *by beasts newly created, breathing vapours.*[8] Therefore that commination of thine, by thy prophet, *I will show wonders in the heaven, and in the earth, blood and fire, and pillars of smoke;*[9] thine apostle, who knew thy meaning best, calls *vapours of smoke.*[10] One prophet presents thee in thy terribleness so, *There went out a smoke at his nostrils,*[11] and another the effect of thine anger so, *The house was filled with smoke;*[12] and he that continues his prophecy as long as the world can continue, describes the miseries of the latter times so, *Out of the bottomless pit arose a smoke, that darkened the sun, and out of that smoke came locusts, who had the power of scorpions.*[13] Now all smokes begin in fire, and all these will end so too: the smoke of sin and of thy wrath will end in the fire of hell. But hast thou afforded us no means to evaporate these smokes, to withdraw these vapours? When thine angels fell from heaven, thou tookest into thy care the reparation of that place, and didst it by assuming, by drawing us thither; when we fell from thee here, in this world, thou tookest into thy care the reparation of this place too, and didst it by assuming us another way, by descending down to assume our nature, in thy Son. So that though our last act be an ascending to glory (we shall ascend to the place of angels), yet our first act is to go the way of thy Son,

[8] Wisd. xi. 18.   [9] Joel, ii. 30.   [10] Acts, ii. 19.
[11] Psalm xviii. 8.   [12] Isaiah, vi. 4.   [13] Rev. ix. 2.

descending, and the way of thy blessed Spirit too, who descended in the dove. Therefore hast thou been pleased to afford us this remedy in nature, by this application of a dove to our lower parts, to make these vapours in our bodies to descend, and to make that a type to us, that, by the visitation of thy Spirit, the vapours of sin shall descend, and we tread them under our feet. At the baptism of thy Son, the Dove descended, and at the exalting of thine apostles to preach, the same Spirit descended. Let us draw down the vapours of our own pride, our own wits, our own wills, our own inventions, to the simplicity of thy sacraments and the obedience of thy word; and these doves, thus applied, shall make us live.

XII. PRAYER.

O ETERNAL and most gracious God, who, though thou have suffered us to destroy ourselves, and hast not given us the power of reparation in ourselves, hast yet afforded us such means of reparation as may easily and familiarly be compassed by us, prosper, I humbly beseech thee, this means of bodily assistance in this thy ordinary creature, and prosper thy means of spiritual assistance in thy holy ordinances. And as thou hast carried this thy creature, the dove, through all thy ways through nature, and made it naturally proper to conduce medicinally to our bodily health, through the law, and made it a sacrifice for sin there, and through the gospel, and made it, and thy Spirit in it, a witness of thy Son's baptism there, so carry it, and the qualities of it, home to my soul, and imprint there that simplicity, that mildness, that harmlessness, which thou hast imprinted by nature in this creature. That so all vapours of all disobedience to thee, being subdued under my feet, I may, in the power and triumph of thy Son, tread victoriously upon my grave, and trample upon the lion and dragon[14] that lie under it to devour me. Thou, O Lord, by the prophet, callest the dove the *dove of the valleys,* but promisest that the *dove of the valleys shall be upon the mountain.*[15] As thou hast laid me low in this valley of sickness, so low as that I am made fit for that question asked in the field of bones, *Son of man, can these bones live?*[16] so, in thy good time, carry me up to these mountains of which even in this valley thou affordest me a prospect, the mountain where thou dwellest, the holy hill, unto which none can ascend *but he that hath clean hands,* which none can have but by that one and that strong way of making them clean, in the blood of thy Son Christ Jesus. Amen.

XIII. Ingeniumque malum, numeroso stigmate, fassus
Pellitur ad pectus, morbique suburbia, morbus.

The sickness declares the infection and malignity thereof by spots.

XIII. MEDITATION.

WE say that the world is made of sea and land, as though they were equal; but we know that there is more sea in the Western than in the Eastern hemisphere. We say that the firmament is full of stars, as though it were equally full; but we know that there are more stars under the Northern than under the Southern pole. We say the elements of man are misery

[14] Psalm xci. 13.   [15] Ezek. vii. 16.   [16] Ezek. xxxvii. 3.

and happiness, as though he had an equal proportion of both, and the days of man vicissitudinary, as though he had as many good days as ill, and that he lived under a perpetual equinoctial, night and day equal, good and ill fortune in the same measure. But it is far from that; he drinks misery, and he tastes happiness; he mows misery, and he gleans happiness; he journeys in misery, he does but walk in happiness; and, which is worst, his misery is positive and dogmatical, his happiness is but disputable and problematical: all men call misery misery, but happiness changes the name by the taste of man. In this accident that befalls me, now that this sickness declares itself by spots to be a malignant and pestilential disease, if there be a comfort in the declaration, that thereby the physicians see more clearly what to do, there may be as much discomfort in this, that the malignity may be so great as that all that they can do shall do nothing; that an enemy declares himself then, when he is able to subsist, and to pursue, and to achieve his ends, is no great comfort. In intestine conspiracies, voluntary confessions do more good than confessions upon the rack; in these infections, when nature herself confesses and cries out by these outward declarations which she is able to put forth of herself, they minister comfort; but when all is by the strength of cordials, it is but a confession upon the rack, by which, though we come to know the malice of that man, yet we do not know whether there be not as much malice in his heart then as before his confession; we are sure of his treason, but not of his repentance; sure of him, but not of his accomplices. It is a faint comfort to know the worst when the worst is remediless, and a weaker than that to know much ill, and not to know that that is the worst. A woman is comforted with the birth of her son, her body is eased of a burden; but if she could prophetically read his history, how ill a man, perchance how ill a son, he would prove, she should receive a greater burden into her mind. Scarce any purchase that is not clogged with secret incumbrances; scarce any happiness that hath not in it so much of the nature of false and base money, as that the allay is more than the metal. Nay, is it not so (at least much towards it) even in the exercise of virtues? I must be poor and want before I can exercise the virtue of gratitude; miserable, and in torment, before I can exercise the virtue of patience. How deep do we dig, and for how coarse gold! And what other touchstone have we of our gold but comparison, whether we be as happy as others, or as ourselves at other times? O poor step toward being well, when these spots do only tell us that we are worse than we were sure of before.

XIII. EXPOSTULATION.

MY God, my God, thou hast made this sick bed thine altar, and I have no other sacrifice to offer but myself; and wilt thou accept no spotted sacrifice? Doth thy Son dwell bodily in this flesh that thou shouldst look for an unspottedness here? or is the Holy Ghost the soul of this body, as he is of thy spouse, who is therefore *all fair, and no spot in her?*[1] or hath thy Son himself no spots, who hath all our stains and deformities in him? or hath thy spouse, thy church, no spots, when every particular limb of that fair and spotless body, every particular soul in that church, is full of stains and spots? Thou bidst us *hate the garment that is spotted with the flesh.*[2] The flesh itself is the garment, and it spotteth itself with itself. And *if I wash myself*

---

[1] Cant. iv. 7.   [2] Jude, 23.

*with snow water, mine own clothes shall make me abomin-
able;*[3] and yet *no man yet ever hated his own flesh.*[4]   Lord,
if thou look for a spotlessness, whom wilt thou look
upon?   Thy mercy may go a great way in my soul and
yet not leave me without spots; thy corrections may go
far and burn deep, and yet not leave me spotless: thy
children apprehended that, when they said, *From our former
iniquity we are not cleansed until this day, though there was
a plague in the congregation of the Lord.*[5]   Thou rainest
upon us, and yet dost not always mollify all our hardness;
thou kindlest thy fires in us, and yet dost not always
burn up all our dross; thou healest our wounds, and yet
leavest scars; thou purgest the blood, and yet leavest spots.
But the spots that thou hatest are the spots that we hide.
The carvers of images cover spots,[6] says the wise man;
when we hide our spots, we become idolators of our own
stains, of our own foulnesses.   But if my spots come forth,
by what means soever, whether by the strength of nature,
by voluntary confession (for grace is the nature of a
regenerate man, and the power of grace is the strength
of nature), or by the virtue of cordials (for even thy
corrections are cordials), if they come forth either way,
thou receivest that confession with a gracious interpretation.   When thy servant Jacob practised an invention
to procure spots in his sheep,[7] thou didst prosper his rods;
and thou dost prosper thine own rods, when corrections
procure the discovery of our spots, the humble manifestation of our sins to thee; till then thou mayst justly
say, *The whole need not the physician;*[8] till we tell thee in
our sickness we think ourselves whole, till we show our
spots, thou appliest no medicine.   But since I do that,
shall I not, *Lord, lift up my face without spot, and be*

---

[3] Job, ix. 30.   [4] Eph. v. 29.   [5] Josh. xxii. 17.
[6] Wisd. xiii. 14.   [7] Gen. xxx. 33.   [8] Matt. ix. 12.

steadfast, and not fear ?[9] Even my spots belong to thy
Son's body, and are part of that which he came down to
this earth to fetch, and challenge, and assume to himself.
When I open my spots I do but present him with that
which is his; and till I do so, I detain and withhold his
right. When therefore thou seest them upon me, as
his, and seest them by this way of confession, they shall
not appear to me as the pinches of death, to decline my
fear to hell (for thou hast not left thy holy one in hell,
thy Son is not there); but these spots upon my breast, and
upon my soul, shall appear to me as the constellations of
the firmament, to direct my contemplation to that place
where thy Son is, thy right hard.

XIII. PRAYER.

O ETERNAL and most gracious God, who as
thou givest all for nothing, if we consider any
precedent merit in us, so givest nothing for
nothing, if we consider the acknowledgment and thankfulness which thou lookest for after, accept my humble
thanks, both for thy mercy, and for this particular mercy,
that in thy judgment I can discern thy mercy, and find
comfort in thy corrections. I know, O Lord, the
ordinary discomfort that accompanies that phrase, that
the house is visited, and that, that thy marks and thy
tokens are upon the patient; but what a wretched and
disconsolate hermitage is that house which is not visited
by thee, and what a waif and stray is that man that hath
not thy marks upon him? These heats, O Lord, which
thou hast brought upon this body, are but thy chafing of
the wax, that thou mightst seal me to thee: these spots are

9 Job, xi. 15.

but the letters in which thou hast written thine own name and conveyed thyself to me; whether for a present possession, by taking me now, or for a future reversion, by glorifying thyself in my stay here, I limit not, I condition not, I choose not, I wish not, no more than the house or land that passeth by any civil conveyance. Only be thou ever present to me, O my God, and this bedchamber and thy bedchamber shall be all one room, and the closing of these bodily eyes here, and the opening of the eyes of my soul there, all one act.

XIV. IDQUE NOTANT CRITICIS MEDICI EVENISSE DIEBUS.

The physicians observe these accidents to have fallen upon the critical days.

XIV. MEDITATION.

I WOULD not make man worse than he is, nor his condition more miserable than it is. But could I though I would? As a man cannot flatter God, nor overpraise him, so a man cannot injure man, nor undervalue him. Thus much must necessarily be presented to his remembrance, that those false happinesses which he hath in this world, have their times, and their seasons, and their critical days; and they are judged and denominated according to the times when they befall us. What poor elements are our happinesses made of, if time, time which we can scarce consider to be any thing, be an essential part of our happiness! All things are done in some place; but if we consider place to be no more but the next hollow superficies of the air, alas! how thin and fluid a thing is air, and how thin a film

88

is a superficies, and a superficies of air! All things are done in time too, but if we consider time to be but the measure of motion, and howsoever it may seem to have three stations, past, present, and future, yet the first and last of these are not (one is not now, and the other is not yet), and that which you call present, is not now the same that it was when you began to call it so in this line (before you sound that word present, or that monosyllable now, the present and the now is past). If this imaginary, half-nothing time, be of the essence of our happinesses, how can they be thought durable? Time is not so; how can they be thought to be? Time is not so; not so considered in any of the parts thereof. If we consider eternity, into that time never entered; eternity is not an everlasting flux of time, but time is a short parenthesis in a long period; and eternity had been the same as it is, though time had never been. If we consider, not eternity, but perpetuity; not that which had no time to begin in, but which shall outlive time, and be when time shall be no more, what a minute is the life of the durablest creature compared to that! and what a minute is man's life in respect of the sun's, or of a tree? and yet how little of our life is occasion, opportunity to receive good in; and how little of that occasion do we apprehend and lay hold of? How busy and perplexed a cobweb is the happiness of man here, that must be made up with a watchfulness to lay hold upon occasion, which is but a little piece of that which is nothing, time? and yet the best things are nothing without that. Honours, pleasures, possessions, presented to us out of time? in our decrepit and distasted and unapprehensive age, lose their office, and lose their name; they are not honours to us that shall never appear, nor come abroad into the eyes of the people, to receive honour from them who give it; nor pleasures to us, who have lost our sense to taste them; nor possessions to us, who are departing from the possession of them. Youth is their critical day, that judges them, that denominates them, that inanimates and informs them, and makes them honours, and pleasures, and possessions; and when they come in an unapprehensive age, they come as a cordial when the bell rings out, as a pardon when the head is off. We rejoice in the comfort of fire, but does any man cleave to it at midsummer? We are glad of the freshness and coolness of a vault, but does any man keep his Christmas there; or are the pleasures of the spring acceptable in autumn? If happiness be in the season, or in the climate, how much happier then are birds than men, who can change the climate and accompany and enjoy the same season ever.

XIV. EXPOSTULATION.

M Y God, my God, wouldst thou call thyself the ancient of days,[1] if we were not to call ourselves to an account for our days? Wouldst thou chide us for *standing idle here all the day*,[2] if we were sure to have more days to make up our harvest? When thou bidst us *take no though tfor to-morrow, for sufficient unto the day* (to every day) *is the evil thereof*,[3] is this truly, absolutely, to put off all that concerns the present life? When thou reprehendest the Galatians by thy message to them, *That they observed days, and months, and times, and years*,[4] when thou sendest by the same messenger to forbid the Colossians all critical days, indicatory days, *Let no man judge you in respect of a holy day, or of a new moon*,

---

[1] Dan. vii. 22.   [2] Matt. xx. 6.   [3] Matt. vi. 34.
[4] Gal. iv. 10.

or of a sabbath[5], dost thou take away all consideration, all distinction of days? Though thou remove them from being of the essence of our salvation, thou leavest them for assistances, and for the exaltation of our devotion, to fix ourselves, at certain periodical and stationary times, upon the consideration of those things which thou hast done for us, and the crisis, the trial, the judgment, how those things have wrought upon us and disposed us to a spiritual recovery and convalescence. For there is to every man a day of salvation. *Now is the accepted time, now is the day of salvation,*[6] and there is *a great day of thy wrath,*[7] which no man shall be able to stand in; and there are evil days before, and therefore thou warnest us and armest us, *Take unto you the whole armour of God, that you may be able to stand in the evil day.*[8] So far then our days must be critical to us, as that by consideration of them, we may make a judgment of our spiritual health, for that is the crisis of our bodily health. Thy beloved servant, St. John, wishes to Gaius, *that he may prosper in his health, so as his soul prospers;*[9] for if the soul be lean the marrow of the body is but water; if the soul wither, the verdure and the good estate of the body is but an illusion and the goodliest man a fearful ghost. Shall we, O my God, determine our thoughts, and shall we never determine our disputations upon our climacterical years, for particular men and periodical years, for the life of states and kingdoms, and never consider these in our long life, and our interest in the everlasting kingdom? We have exercised our curiosity in observing that Adam, the eldest of the eldest world, died in his climacterical year, and Shem, the eldest son of the next world, in his; Abraham, the father of the faithful, in his, and the

[5] Col. ii. 16. [6] 2 Cor. vi. 2. [7] Rev. vi. 17.
[8] Eph. vi. 11. [9] 3 John, 2.

blessed Virgin Mary, the garden where the root of faith grew, in hers. But they whose climacterics we observe, employed their observation upon their critical days, the working of thy promise of a Messias upon them. And shall we, O my God, make less use of those days who have more of them? We, who have not only the day of the prophets, the first days, but the last days, in which thou hast spoken unto us by thy Son?[10] We are the children of the day,[11] for thou hast shined in as full a noon upon us as upon the Thessalonians: they who were of the night (a night which they had superinduced upon themselves), the Pharisees, pretended, *that if they had been in their fathers' days* (those indicatory and judicatory, those critical days), *they would not have been partakers of the blood of the prophets;*[12] and shall we who are in the day, these days, not of the prophets, but of the Son, stone those prophets again, and crucify that Son again, for all those evident indications and critical judicatures which are afforded us? Those opposed adversaries of thy Son, the Pharisees, with the Herodians, watched a critical day; then when the state was incensed against him, came to tempt him in the dangerous question of tribute.[13] They left him, and that day was the critical day to the Sadducees. The same day, says thy Spirit in thy word, the Sadducees came to him to question him about the resurrection,[14] and them he silenced; they left him, and this was the critical day for the Scribe, expert in the law, who thought himself learneder than the Herodian, the Pharisee, or Sadducee; and he tempted him about the great commandment,[15] and him Christ left without power of replying. When all was done, and that they went about to begin their circle of vexation and temptation again,

[10] Heb. i. 2. [11] 1 Thes. v. 8. [12] Matt. xxiii. 30.
[13] Matt. xxii. 15. [14] Matt. xxii. 23. [15] Matt. xxii. 36.

Christ silences them so, that as they had taken their critical days, to come in that and in that day, so Christ imposes a critical day upon them. *From that day forth, says thy Spirit, no man durst ask him any more questions.*[16] This, O my God, my most blessed God, is a fearful crisis, a fearful indication, when we will study, and seek, and find, what days are fittest to forsake thee in; to say, now religion is in a neutrality in the world, and this is my day, the day of liberty; now I may make new friends by changing my old religion, and this is my day, the day of advancement. But, O my God, with thy servant Jacob's holy boldness, who, though thou lamedst him, would not let thee go till thou hadst given him a blessing;[17] though thou have laid me upon my hearse, yet thou shalt not depart from me, from this bed, till thou have given me a crisis, a judgment upon myself this day. Since *a day is as a thousand years with thee,*[18] let, O Lord, a day be as a week to me; and in this one, let me consider seven days, seven critical days, and judge myself that I be not judged by thee. First, this is the day of thy visitation, thy coming to me; and would I look to be welcome to thee, and not entertain thee in thy coming to me? We measure not the visitations of great persons by their apparel, by their equipage, by the solemnity of their coming, but by their very coming; and therefore, howsoever thou come, it is a crisis to me, that thou wouldst not lose me who seekest me by any means. This leads me from my first day, thy visitation by sickness, to a second, to the light and testimony of my conscience. There I have an evening and a morning, a sad guiltiness in my soul, but yet a cheerful rising of thy Sun too; thy evenings and mornings made days in the creation, and there is no mention of nights; my sadnesses for sins are evenings, but

[16] Matt. xxii. 46. [17] Gen. xxxii. 26. [18] 2 Pet. iii. 8.

they determine not in night, but deliver me over to the day, the day of a conscience dejected, but then rectified, accused, but then acquitted, by thee, by him who speaks thy word, and who is thy word, thy Son. From this day, the crisis and examination of my conscience, breaks out my third day, my day of preparing and fitting myself for a more especial receiving of thy Son in his institution of the Sacrament; in which day, though there be many dark passages and slippery steps to them who will entangle and endanger themselves in unnecessary disputations, yet there are light hours enough for any man to go his whole journey intended by thee, to know that that bread and wine is not more really assimilated to my body, and to my blood, than the body and blood of thy Son is communicated to me in that action, and participation of that bread and that wine. And having, O my God, walked with thee these three days, the day of thy visitation, the day of my conscience, the day of preparing for this seal of reconciliation, I am the less afraid of the clouds or storms of my fourth day, the day of my dissolution and transmigration from hence. Nothing deserves the name of happiness that makes the remembrance of death bitter; and, *O death, how bitter is the remembrance of thee, to a man that lives at rest in his possessions, the man that hath nothing to vex him, yea unto him that is able to receive meat !*[19] Therefore hast thou, O my God, made this sickness, in which I am not able to receive meat, my fasting day, my eve to this great festival, my dissolution. And this day of death shall deliver me over to my fifth day, the day of my resurrection; for how long a day soever thou make that day in the grave, yet there is no day between that and the resurrection. Then we shall all be invested, reapparelled in our own bodies; but they

[19] Ecclus. xli. 1.

who have made just use of their former days be super-
invested with glory; whereas the others, condemned to
their old clothes, their sinful bodies, shall have nothing
added but immortality to torment.   And this day of
awaking me, and reinvesting my soul in my body, and
my body in the body of Christ, shall present me, body and
soul, to my sixth day, the day of judgment, which is
truly, and most literally, the critical, the decretory day;
both because all judgment shall be manifested to me
then, and I shall assist in judging the world then, and
because then, that judgment shall declare to me, and
possess me of my seventh day, my everlasting Sabbath
in thy rest, thy glory, thy joy, thy sight, thyself; and
where I shall live as long without reckoning any more
days after, as thy Son and thy Holy Spirit lived with
thee, before you three made any days in the creation.

XIV.   PRAYER.

O ETERNAL and most gracious God, who,
though thou didst permit darkness to be before
light in the creation, yet in the making of light
didst so multiply that light, as that it enlightened not
the day only, but the night too; though thou have suffered
some dimness, some clouds of sadness and disconsolateness
to shed themselves upon my soul, I humbly bless and
thankfully glorify thy holy name, that thou hast afforded
me the light of thy Spirit, against which the prince of
darkness cannot prevail, nor hinder his illumination of
our darkest nights, of our saddest thoughts.   Even the
visitation of thy most blessed Spirit upon the blessed
Virgin, is called an overshadowing. There was the
presence of the Holy Ghost, the fountain of all light,

and yet an overshadowing; nay, except there were some light, there could be no shadow. Let thy merciful providence so govern all in this sickness, that I never fall into utter darkness, ignorance of thee, or inconsideration of myself; and let those shadows which do fall upon me, faintnesses of spirit, and condemnations of myself, be overcome by the power of thine irresistible light, the God of consolation; that when those shadows have done their office upon me, to let me see, that of myself I should fall into irrecoverable darkness, thy Spirit may do his office upon those shadows, and disperse them, and establish me in so bright a day here, as may be a critical day to me, a day wherein and whereby I may give thy judgment upon myself, and that the words of thy Son, spoken to his apostles, may reflect upon me, *Behold, I am with you always, even to the end of the world.*[20]

XV.   Interea insomnes noctes ego duco, diesque.

I sleep not day nor night.

XV.   MEDITATION.

NATURAL men have conceived a twofold use of sleep; that it is a refreshing of the body in this life; that it is a preparing of the soul for the next; that it is a feast, and it is the grace at that feast; that it is our recreation and cheers us, and it is our catechism and instructs us; we lie down in a hope that we shall rise the stronger, and we lie down in a knowledge that we may rise no more.   Sleep is an opiate which gives us rest, but such an opiate, as perchance, being under it, we

[20] Matt. xxviii. 20.

shall wake no more. But though natural men, who have induced secondary and figurative considerations, have found out this second, this emblematical use of sleep, that it should be a representation of death, God, who wrought and perfected his work before nature began (for nature was but his apprentice, to learn in the first seven days, and now is his foreman, and works next under him), God, I say, intended sleep only for the refreshing of man by bodily rest, and not for a figure of death, for he intended not death itself then. But man having induced death upon himself, God hath taken man's creature, death, into his hand, and mended it; and whereas it hath in itself a fearful form and aspect, so that man is afraid of his own creature, God presents it to him in a familiar, in an assiduous, in an agreeable and acceptable form, in sleep; that so when he awakes from sleep, and says to himself, " Shall I be no otherwise when I am dead, than I was even now when I was asleep? " he may be ashamed of his waking dreams, and of his melancholy fancying out a horrid and an affrightful figure of that death which is so like sleep. As then we need sleep to live out our threescore and ten years, so we need death to live that life which we cannot outlive. And as death being our enemy, God allows us to defend ourselves against it (for we victual ourselves against death twice every day), as often as we eat, so God having so sweetened death unto us as he hath in sleep, we put ourselves into our enemy's hands once every day, so far as sleep is death; and sleep is as much death as meat is life. This then is the misery of my sickness, that death, as it is produced from me and is mine own creature, is now before mine eyes, but in that form in which God hath mollified it to us, and made it acceptable, in sleep I cannot see it. How many prisoners, who have even hollowed themselves their graves upon that earth on which they have lain long under heavy fetters, yet at this hour are asleep, though they be yet working upon their own graves by their own weight? He that hath seen his friend die to-day, or knows he shall see it to-morrow, yet will sink into a sleep between. I cannot, and oh, if I be entering now into eternity, where there shall be no more distinction of hours, why is it all my business now to tell clocks? Why is none of the heaviness of my heart dispensed into mine eye-lids, that they might fall as my heart doth? And why, since I have lost my delight in all objects, cannot I discontinue the faculty of seeing them by closing mine eyes in sleep? But why rather, being entering into that presence where I shall wake continually and never sleep more, do I not interpret my continual waking here, to be a parasceve and a preparation to that?

XV. EXPOSTULATION.

MY God, my God, I know (for thou hast said it) that *he that keepeth Israel shall neither slumber nor sleep:*[1] but shall not that Israel, over whom thou watchest, sleep? I know (for thou hast said it) that there are men whose damnation sleepeth not;[2] but shall not they to whom thou art salvation sleep? or wilt thou take from them that evidence, and that testimony that they are thy Israel, or thou their salvation? *Thou givest thy beloved sleep:*[3] shall I lack that seal of thy love? *You shall lie down, and none shall make you afraid:*[4] shall I be outlawed from that protection? Jonah slept in

---

[1] Psalm cxxi. 4.   [2] 2 Pet. ii. 3.   [3] Psalm cxxvii. 2.
[4] Lev. xxvi. 6.

one dangerous storm,[5] and thy blessed Son in another;[6] shall I have no use, no benefit, no application of those great examples? *Lord, if he sleep, he shall do well,*[7] say thy Son's disciples to him of Lazarus; and shall there be no room for that argument in me? or shall I be open to the contrary? If I sleep not, shall I not be well in their sense? Let me not, O my God, take this too precisely, too literally; *There is that neither day nor night seeth sleep with his eyes,*[8] says thy wise servant Solomon; and whether he speak that of worldly men, or of men that seek wisdom, whether in justification or condemnation of their watchfulness, we cannot tell: we can tell that there are men that cannot sleep till they have done mischief,[9] and then they can; and we can tell that the rich man cannot sleep, because his abundance will not let him.[10]   The tares were sown when the husbandmen were asleep[11]; and the elders thought it a probable excuse, a credible lie, that the watchmen which kept the sepulchre should say, that the body of thy Son was stolen away when they were asleep.[12]   Since thy blessed Son rebuked his disciples for sleeping, shall I murmur because I do not sleep? If Samson had slept any longer in Gaza, he had been taken;[13] and when he did sleep longer with Delilah,[14] he was taken. Sleep is as often taken for natural death in thy Scriptures, as for natural rest. Nay, sometimes sleep hath so heavy a sense, as to be taken for sin itself,[15] as well as for the punishment of sin, death.[16] Much comfort is not in much sleep, when the most fearful and most irrevocable malediction is presented by thee in a perpetual sleep. *I will make their feasts, and I*

---

[5] Jonah, i. 5.   [6] Matt. viii. 24.   [7] John, xi. 12.
[8] Eccles. viii. 16.   [9] Prov. iv. 16.   [10] Eccles. v. 12.
[11] Matt. xiii. 25; xxviii. 13.   [12] Matt. xxvi. 40.
[13] Judges, xvi. 3.   [14] Judges, xvi. 19.   [15] Eph. v. 14.
[16] 1 Thes. v. 6.

will make them drunk, and they shall sleep a perpetual sleep, and not wake.[17]   I must therefore, O my God, look farther than into the very act of sleeping before I misinterpret my waking; for since I find thy whole hand light, shall any finger of that hand seem heavy?   Since the whole sickness is thy physic, shall any accident in it be my poison by my murmuring?   The name of watchmen belongs to our profession; thy prophets are not only seers, endued with a power of seeing, able to see, but watchmen evermore in the act of seeing.   And therefore give me leave, O my blessed God, to invert the words of thy Son's spouse: she said, *I sleep, but my heart waketh;*[18] I say, I wake, but my heart sleepeth: my body is in a sick weariness, but my soul in a peaceful rest with thee; and as our eyes in our health see not the air that is next them, nor the fire, nor the spheres, nor stop upon any thing till they come to stars, so my eyes that are open, see nothing of this world, but pass through all that, and fix themselves upon thy peace, and joy, and glory above. Almost as soon as thy apostle had said, *Let us not sleep,*[19] lest we should be too much discomforted if we did, he says again, *Whether we wake or sleep, let us live together with Christ.*[20]   Though then this absence of sleep may argue the presence of death (the original may exclude the copy, the life the picture), yet this gentle sleep and rest of my soul betroths me to thee, to whom I shall be married indissolubly, though by this way of dissolution.

[17] Jer. li. 57.   [18] Cant. v. 2.   [19] 1 Thes. v. 6.
[20] 1 Thes. v. 10.

XV. PRAYER.

O ETERNAL and most gracious God, who art able to make, and dost make, the sick bed of thy servants chapels of ease to them, and the dreams of thy servants prayers and meditations upon thee, let not this continual watchfulness of mine, this inability to sleep, which thou hast laid upon me, be any disquiet or discomfort to me, but rather an argument, that thou wouldst not have me sleep in thy presence. What it may indicate or signify concerning the state of my body, let them consider to whom that consideration belongs; do thou, who only art the Physician of my soul, tell her, that thou wilt afford her such defensatives, as that she shall wake ever towards thee, and yet ever sleep in thee, and that, through all this sickness, thou wilt either preserve mine understanding from all decays and distractions which these watchings might occasion, or that thou wilt reckon and account with me from before those violences, and not call any piece of my sickness a sin. It is a heavy and indelible sin that I brought into the world with me; it is a heavy and innumerable multitude of sins which I have heaped up since; I have sinned behind thy back (if that can be done), by wilful abstaining from thy congregations and omitting thy service, and I have sinned before thy face, in my hypocrisies in prayer, in my ostentation, and the mingling a respect of myself in preaching thy word; I have sinned in my fasting, by repining when a penurious fortune hath kept me low; and I have sinned even in that fulness, when I have been at thy table, by a negligent examination, by a wilful prevarication, in receiving that heavenly food and physic. But as I know, O my gracious God, that for all those sins committed since, yet thou wilt consider me, as I was in thy purpose when thou wrotest my name in the book of life in mine election; so into what deviations soever I stray and wander by occasion of this sickness, O God, return thou to that minute wherein thou wast pleased with me and consider me in that condition.

XVI.   ET PROPERARE MEUM CLAMANT, E TURRE PROPINQUA, OBSTREPERÆ CAMPANÆ ALIORUM IN FUNERE, FUNUS.

From the bells of the church adjoining, I am daily remembered of my burial in the funerals of others.

XVI. MEDITATION.

WE have a convenient author,[1] who writ a discourse of bells when he was prisoner in Turkey.   How would he have enlarged himself if he had been my fellow-prisoner in this sick bed, so near to that steeple which never ceases, no more than the harmony of the spheres, but is more heard.   When the Turks took Constantinople, they melted the bells into ordnance; I have heard both bells and ordnance, but never been so much affected with those as with these bells.   I have lain near a steeple[2] in which there are said to be more than thirty bells, and near another, where there is one so big, as that the clapper is said to weigh more than six hundred pounds,[3] yet never so affected as here.   Here the bells can scarce solemnize the funeral of any person, but that I knew him, or knew that he was my neighbour: we dwelt in houses near to one another before, but now he is gone into that house into which I must follow him.   There

---

[1] Magius.   [2] Antwerp.   [3] Roan.

is a way of correcting the children of great persons, that other children are corrected in their behalf, and in their names, and this works upon them who indeed had more deserved it. And when these bells tell me, that now one, and now another is buried, must not I acknowledge that they have the correction due to me, and paid the debt that I owe? There is a story of a bell in a monastery[4] which, when any of the house was sick to death, rung always voluntarily, and they knew the inevitableness of the danger by that. It rung once when no man was sick, but the next day one of the house fell from the steeple and died, and the bell held the reputation of a prophet still. If these bells that warn to a funeral now, were appropriated to none, may not I, by the hour of the funeral, supply? How many men that stand at an execution, if they would ask, For what dies that man? should hear their own faults condemned, and see themselves executed by attorney? We scarce hear of any man preferred, but we think of ourselves that we might very well have been that man; why might not I have been that man that is carried to his grave now? Could I fit myself to stand or sit in any man's place, and not to lie in any man's grave? I may lack much of the good parts of the meanest, but I lack nothing of the mortality of the weakest; they may have acquired better abilities than I, but I was born to as many infirmities as they. To be an incumbent by lying down in a grave, to be a doctor by teaching mortification by example, by dying, though I may have seniors, others may be older than I, yet I have proceeded apace in a good university, and gone a great way in a little time, by the furtherance of a vehement fever, and whomsoever these bells bring to the ground to-day, if he and I had been compared yesterday, perchance

---

[4] Roccha.

I should have been thought likelier to come to this preferment then than he. God hath kept the power of death in his own hands, lest any man should bribe death. If man knew the gain of death, the ease of death, he would solicit, he would provoke death to assist him by any hand which he might use. But as when men see many of their own professions preferred, it ministers a hope that that may light upon them; so when these hourly bells tell me of so many funerals of men like me, it presents, if not a desire that it may, yet a comfort whensoever mine shall come.

XVI. EXPOSTULATION.

MY God, my God, I do not expostulate with thee, but with them who dare do that; who dare expostulate with thee, when in the voice of thy church thou givest allowance to this ceremony of bells at funerals. Is it enough to refuse it, because it was in use among the Gentiles? so were funerals too. Is it because some abuses may have crept in amongst Christians? Is that enough, that their ringing hath been said to drive away evil spirits? Truly, that is so far true, as that the evil spirit is vehemently vexed in their ringing, therefore, because that action brings the congregation together, and unites God and his people, to the destruction of that kingdom which the evil spirit usurps. In the first institution of thy church in this world, in the foundation of thy militant church amongst the Jews, thou didst appoint the calling of the assembly in to be by trumpet;[5] and when they were in, then thou gavest them the sound of bells in the garment of thy priest.[6] In the triumphan

[5] Numb. x. 2.   [6] Exod. xviii. 33-4.

church, thou employest both too, but in an inverted order; we enter into the triumphant church by the sound of bells (for we enter when we die); and then we receive our further edification, or consummation, by the sound of trumpets at the resurrection. The sound of thy trumpets thou didst impart to secular and civil uses too, but the sound of bells only to sacred. Lord, let not us break the communion of saints in that which was intended for the advancement of it; let not that pull us asunder from one another, which was intended for the assembling of us in the militant, and associating of us to the triumphant church. But he, for whose funeral these bells ring now, was at home, at his journey's end yesterday; why ring they now? A man, that is a world, is all the things in the world; he is an army, and when an army marches, the van may lodge to-night where the rear comes not till to-morrow. A man extends to his act and to his example; to that which he does, and that which he teaches; so do those things that concern him, so do these bells; that which rung yesterday was to convey him out of the world in his van, in his soul; that which rung to-day was to bring him in his rear, in his body, to the church; and this continuing of ringing after his entering is to bring him to me in the application. Where I lie I could hear the psalm, and did join with the congregation in it; but I could not hear the sermon, and these latter bells are a repetition sermon to me. But, O my God, my God, do I that have this fever need other remembrances of my mortality? Is not mine own hollow voice, voice enough to pronounce that to me? Need I look upon a death's head in a ring, that have one in my face? or go for death to my neighbour's house, that have him in my bosom? We cannot, we cannot, O my God, take in too many helps for religious duties; I know I cannot have any better image of thee than thy Son, nor any better image of him than his Gospel; yet must not I with thanks confess to thee, that some historical pictures of his have sometimes put me upon better meditations than otherwise I should have fallen upon? I know thy church needed not to have taken in, from Jew, or Gentile, any supplies for the exaltation of thy glory, or our devotion; of absolute necessity I know she needed not; but yet we owe thee our thanks, that thou hast given her leave to do so, and that as, in making us Christians, thou didst not destroy that which we were before, natural men, so, in the exalting of our religious devotions now we are Christians, thou hast been pleased to continue to us those assistances which did work upon the affections of natural men before; for thou lovest a good man as thou lovest a good Christian; and though grace be merely from me, yet thou dost not plant grace but in good natures.

XVI. PRAYER.

O ETERNAL and most gracious God, who having consecrated our living bodies to thine own Spirit, and made us temples of the Holy Ghost, dost also require a respect to be given to these temples, even when the priest is gone out of them, to these bodies when the soul is departed from them, I bless and glorify thy name, that as thou takest care in our life of every hair of our head, so dost thou also of every grain of ashes after our death. Neither dost thou only do good to us all in life and death, but also wouldst have us do good to one another, as in a holy life, so in those things which accompany our death. In that contemplation I make account that I hear this dead brother of ours, who is now carried out to his burial, to speak to me, and to preach my funeral sermon in the voice of these bells.   In him, O God, thou hast accomplished to me even the request of Dives to Abraham; thou hast sent one from the dead to speak unto me.   He speaks to me aloud from that steeple; he whispers to me at these curtains, and he speaks thy words: *Blessed are the dead which die in the Lord from henceforth.*[7]   Let this prayer therefore, O my God, be as my last gasp, my expiring, my dying in thee; that if this be the hour of my transmigration, I may die the death of a sinner, drowned in my sins, in the blood of thy Son; and if I live longer, yet I may now die the death of the righteous, die to sin; which death is a resurrection to a new life.   *Thou killest and thou givest life:* whichsoever comes, it comes from thee; which way soever it comes, let me come to thee.

XVII. Nunc lento sonitu dicunt, morieris.

Now, this bell tolling softly for another, says to me:
Thou must die.

XVII. MEDITATION.

PERCHANCE he for whom this bell tolls may be so ill, as that he knows not it tolls for him; and perchance I may think myself so much better than I am, as that they who are about me, and see my state, may have caused it to toll for me, and I know not that. The church is Catholic, universal, so are all her actions; all that she does belongs to all.   When she baptizes a child, that action concerns me; for that child is thereby connected to that body which is my head too,   and ingrafted

[7] Rev. xiv. 13.

into that body whereof I am a member. And when she buries a man, that action concerns me: all mankind is of one author, and is one volume; when one man dies, one chapter is not torn out of the book, but translated into a better language; and every chapter must be so translated; God employs several translators; some pieces are translated by age, some by sickness, some by war, some by justice; but God's hand is in every translation, and his hand shall bind up all our scattered leaves again for that library where every book shall lie open to one another. As therefore the bell that rings to a sermon calls not upon the preacher only, but upon the congregation to come, so this bell calls us all; but how much more me, who am brought so near the door by this sickness. There was a contention as far as a suit (in which both piety and dignity, religion and estimation, were mingled), which of the religious orders should ring to prayers first in the morning; and it was determined, that they should ring first that rose earliest. If we understand aright the dignity of this bell that tolls for our evening prayer, we would be glad to make it ours by rising early, in that application, that it might be ours as well as his, whose indeed it is. The bell doth toll for him that thinks it doth; and though it intermit again, yet from that minute that that occasion wrought upon him, he is united to God. Who casts not up his eye to the sun when it rises? but who takes off his eye from a comet when that breaks out? Who bends not his ear to any bell which upon any occasion rings? but who can remove it from that bell which is passing a piece of himself out of this world? No man is an island, entire of itself; every man is a piece of the continent, a part of the main. If a clod be washed away by the sea, Europe is the less, as well as if a promontory were, as well as if a manor of thy friend's or of thine

108

own were: any man's death diminishes me, because I am involved in mankind, and therefore never send to know for whom the bells tolls; it tolls for thee. Neither can we call this a begging of misery, or a borrowing of misery, as though we were not miserable enough of ourselves, but must fetch in more from the next house, in taking upon us the misery of our neighbours. Truly it were an excusable covetousness if we did, for affliction is a treasure, and scarce any man hath enough of it. No man hath affliction enough that is not matured and ripened by it, and made fit for God by that affliction. If a man carry treasure in bullion, or in a wedge of gold, and have none coined into current money, his treasure will not defray him as he travels. Tribulation is treasure in the nature of it, but it is not current money in the use of it, except we get nearer and nearer our home, heaven, by it. Another man may be sick too, and sick to death, and this affliction may lie in his bowels, as gold in a mine, and be of no use to him; but this bell, that tells me of his affliction, digs out and applies that gold to me: if by this consideration of another's danger I take mine own into contemplation, and so secure myself, by making my recourse to my God, who is our only security.

XVII. EXPOSTULATION.

MY God, my God, is this one of thy ways of drawing light out of darkness, to make him for whom this bell tolls, now in this dimness of his sight, to become a superintendent, an overseer, a bishop, to as many as hear his voice in this bell, and to give us a confirmation in this action? Is this one of thy ways, to raise strength out of weakness, to make him who cannot rise from his bed, nor stir in his bed, come home to me, and in this sound give me the strength of healthy and vigorous instructions? O my God, my God, what thunder is not a well-tuned cymbal, what hoarseness, what harshness, is not a clear organ, if thou be pleased to set thy voice to it? And what organ is not well played on if thy hand be upon it? Thy voice, thy hand, is in this sound, and in this one sound I hear this whole concert. I hear thy Jacob call unto his sons and say, *Gather your-selves together, that I may tell you what shall befall you in the last days:*[1] he says, That which I am now, you must be then. I hear thy Moses telling me, and all within the compass of this sound, *This is the blessing wherewith I bless you before my death;*[2] this, that before your death, you would consider your own in mine. I hear thy prophet saying to Hezekiah, *Set thy house in order, for thou shalt die, and not live :*[3] he makes use of his family, and calls this a setting of his house in order, to compose us to the meditation of death. I hear thy apostle saying, *I think it meet to put you in remembrance, knowing that shortly I must go out of this tabernacle :*[4] this is the publishing of his will, and this bell is our legacy, the applying of his present condition to our use. I hear that which makes all sounds music, and all music perfect; I hear thy Son himself saying, *Let not your hearts be troubled;*[5] only I hear this change, that whereas thy Son says there, *I go to prepare a place for you*, this man in this sound says, I send to prepare you for a place, for a grave. But, O my God, my God, since heaven is glory and joy, why do not glorious and joyful things lead us, induce us to heaven? Thy legacies in thy first will, in the Old Testament, were plenty and victory, wine and oil, milk and honey,

[1] Gen. xlix. 1.   [2] Deut. xxxiii. 1.   [3] 2 Kings, xx. 1.
[4] 2 Pet. i. 13.   [5] John, xiv. 1.

alliances of friends, ruin of enemies, peaceful hearts and cheerful countenances, and by these galleries thou broughtest them into thy bedchamber, by these glories and joys, to the joys and glories of heaven. Why hast thou changed thine old way, and carried us by the ways of discipline and mortification, by the ways of mourning and lamentation, by the ways of miserable ends and miserable anticipations of those miseries, in appropriating the exemplar miseries of others to ourselves, and usurping upon their miseries as our own, to our prejudice? Is the glory of heaven no perfecter in itself, but that it needs a foil of depression and ingloriousness in this world, to set it off? Is the joy of heaven no perfecter in itself, but that it needs the sourness of this life to give it a taste? Is that joy and that glory but a comparative glory and a comparative joy? not such in itself, but such in comparison of the joylessness and the ingloriousness of this world? I know, my God, it is far, far otherwise. As thou thyself, who art all, art made of no substances, so the joys and glory which are with thee are made of none of these circumstances, essential joy, and glory essential. But why then, my God, wilt thou not begin them here? Pardon, O God, this unthankful rashness; I that ask why thou dost not, find even now in myself, that thou dost; such joy, such glory, as that I conclude upon myself, upon all, they that find not joys in their sorrows, glory in their dejections in this world, are in a fearful danger of missing both in the next.

XVII. PRAYER.

O ETERNAL and most gracious God, who hast been pleased to speak to us, not only in the voice of nature, who speaks in our hearts, and of thy word, which speaks to our ears, but in the speech of peechless creatures, in Balaam's ass, in the speech of unbelieving men, in the confession of Pilate, in the speech of the devil himself, in the recognition and attestation of thy Son, I humbly accept thy voice in the sound of this sad and funeral bell. And first, I bless thy glorious name, that in this sound and voice I can hear thy instructions, in another man's to consider mine own condition; and to know, that this bell which tolls for another, before it come to ring out, may take me in too. As death is the wages of sin it is due to me; as death is the end of sickness it belongs to me; and though so disobedient a servant as I may be afraid to die, yet to so merciful a master as thou I cannot be afraid to come; and therefore into thy hands, O my God, I commend my spirit, a surrender which I know thou wilt accept, whether I live or die; for thy servant David made it,[6] when he put himself into thy protection for his life; and thy blessed Son made it, when he delivered up his soul at his death: declare thou thy will upon me, O Lord, for life or death in thy time; receive my surrender of myself now; into thy hands, O Lord, I commend my spirit. And being thus, O my God, prepared by thy correction, mellowed by thy chastisement, and conformed to thy will by thy Spirit, having received thy pardon for my soul, and asking no reprieve for my body, I am bold, O Lord, to bend my prayers to thee for his assistance, the voice of whose bell

[6] Psalm xxxi. 5.

hath called me to this devotion. Lay hold upon his soul, O God, till that soul have thoroughly considered his account; and how few minutes soever it have to remain in that body, let the power of thy Spirit recompense the shortness of time, and perfect his account before he pass away; present his sins so to him, as that he may know what thou forgivest, and not doubt of thy forgiveness, let him stop upon the infiniteness of those sins, but dwell upon the infiniteness of thy mercy; let him discern his own demerits, but wrap himself up in the merits of thy Son Christ Jesus; breathe inward comforts to his heart, and afford him the power of giving such outward testimonies thereof, as all that are about him may derive comforts from thence, and have this edification, even in this dissolution, that though the body be going the way of all flesh, yet that soul is going the way of all saints. When thy Son cried out upon the cross, *My God, my God, why hast thou forsaken me?* he spake not so much in his own person, as in the person of the church, and of his afflicted members, who in deep distresses might fear thy forsaking. This patient, O most blessed God, is one of them; in his behalf, and in his name, hear thy Son crying to thee, *My God, my God, why hast thou forsaken me?* and forsake him not; but with thy left hand lay his body in the grave (if that be thy determination upon him), and with thy right hand receive his soul into thy kingdom, and unite him and us in one communion of saints. Amen.

XVIII. ——————————————— At inde
Mortuus es, sonitu celeri, pulsuque agitato.

The bell rings out, and tells me in him, that I am dead.

XVIII. MEDITATION.

THE bell rings out, the pulse thereof is changed; the tolling was a faint and intermitting pulse, upon one side; this stronger, and argues more and better life. His soul is gone out, and as a man who had a lease of one thousand years after the expiration of a short one, or an inheritance after the life of a man in a consumption, he is now entered into the possession of his better estate. His soul is gone, whither? Who saw it come in, or who saw it go out? Nobody; yet everybody is sure he had one, and hath none. If I will ask mere philosophers what the soul is, I shall find amongst them that will tell me, it is nothing but the temperament and harmony, and just and equal composition of the elements in the body, which produces all those faculties which we ascribe to the soul; and so in itself is nothing, no separable substance that overlives the body. They see the soul is nothing else in other creatures, and they affect an impious humility to think as low of man. But if my soul were no more than the soul of a beast, I could not think so; that soul that can reflect upon itself, consider itself, is more than so. If I will ask, not mere philosophers, but mixed men, philosophical divines, how the soul, being a separate substance, enters into man, I shall find some that will tell me, that it is by generation and procreation from parents, because they think it hard to charge the soul with the guiltiness of original sin if the soul were infused into a body in which it must necessarily grow foul, and contract original sin whether it will or no; and I shall find some that will tell me, that it is by immediate infusion from God, because they think it hard to maintain an immortality in such a soul, as should be begotten and derived with the body from mortal parents. If I will ask, not a few men, but almost whole bodies, whole churches, what becomes of the souls of the righteous at the departing thereof from the body, I shall be told by some, that they attend an expiation, a purification in a place of torment; by some, that they attend the fruition of the sight of God in a place of rest, but yet but of expectation; by some, that they pass to an immediate possession of the presence of God. St. Augustine studied the nature of the soul as much as any thing, but the salvation of the soul; and he sent an express messenger to St. Hierome, to consult of some things concerning the soul; but he satisfies himself with this: "Let the departure of my soul to salvation be evident to my faith, and I care the less how dark the entrance of my soul into my body be to my reason." It is the going out, more than the coming in, that concerns us. This soul this bell tells me is gone out, whither? Who shall tell me that? I know not who it is, much less what he was, the condition of the man, and the course of his life, which should tell me whither he is gone, I know not. I was not there in his sickness, nor at his death; I saw not his way nor his end, nor can ask them who did, thereby to conclude or argue whither he is gone. But yet I have one nearer me than all these, mine own charity; I ask that, and that tells me he is gone to everlasting rest, and joy, and glory. I owe him a good opinion; it is but thankful charity in me, because I received benefit and instruction from him when his bell tolled; and I, being made the fitter to pray by that disposition, wherein I was assisted by his occasion, did pray for him; and I pray not without faith; so I do charitably, so I do faithfully believe, that that soul is gone to everlasting rest, and joy, and glory. But for the body, how poor a wretched thing is that? we cannot express it so fast, as it grows worse and worse. That body, which scarce three minutes since was such a house, as that that soul, which made but one step from thence to heaven, was scarce thoroughly content to leave that for heaven; that body hath lost the name of a dwelling-house, because none dwells in it, and is making haste to lose the name of a body, and dissolve to putrefaction. Who would not be affected to see a clear and sweet river in the morning, grow a kennel of muddy land-water by noon, and condemned to the saltness of the sea by night? and how lame a picture, how faint a representation is that, of the precipitation of man's body to dissolution? Now all the parts built up, and knit by a lovely soul, now but a statue of clay, and now these limbs melted off, as if that clay were but snow; and now the whole house is but a handful of sand, so much dust, and but a peck of rubbish, so much bone. If he who, as this bell tells me, is gone now, were some excellent artificer, who comes to him for a cloak or for a garment now? or for counsel, if he were a lawyer? if a magistrate, for justice? Man, before he hath his immortal soul, hath a soul of sense, and a soul of vegetation before that: this immortal soul did not forbid other souls to be in us before, but when this soul departs, it carries all with it; no more vegetation, no more sense. Such a mother-in-law is the earth, in respect of our natural mother; in her womb we grew, and when she was delivered of us, we were planted in some place, in some calling in the world; in the womb of the earth we diminish, and when she is delivered of us, our grave opened for another; we are not transplanted,

116

but transported, our dust blown away with profane dust, with every wind.

XVIII. EXPOSTULATION.

MY God, my God, if expostulation be too bold a word, do thou mollify it with another; let it be wonder in myself, let it be but problem to others; but let me ask, why wouldst thou not suffer those that serve thee in holy services, to do any office about the dead,[1] nor assist at their funeral? Thou hadst no counsellor, thou needst none; thou hast no controller, thou admittedst none. Why do I ask? In ceremonial things (as that was) any convenient reason is enough; who can be sure to propose that reason, that moved thee in the institution thereof? I satisfy myself with this; that in those times the Gentiles were over-full of an over-reverent respect to the memory of the dead: a great part of the idolatry of the nations flowed from that; an over-amorous devotion, an over-zealous celebrating, and over-studious preserving of the memories, and the pictures of some dead persons; and by *the vain glory of men, they entered into the world*,[2] and their statues and pictures contracted an opinion of divinity by age: that which was at first but a picture of a friend grew a god in time, as the wise man notes, *They called them gods, which were the work of an ancient hand*.[3] And some have assigned a certain time, when a picture should come out of minority, and be at age to be a god in sixty years after it is made. Those images of men that had life, and some idols of other things which never had any being, are by one common name called promiscuously dead; and for that the wise

---

[1] Levit. xxi. 1. [2] Wisd. xiv. 14. [3] Wisd. xiii. 10.

man reprehends the idolater, *for health he prays to that which is weak, and for life he prays to that which is dead.*[4] Should we do so? says thy prophet;[5] *should we go from the living to the dead ?* So much ill then being occasioned by so much religious compliment exhibited to the dead, thou, O God (I think), wouldst therefore inhibit thy principal holy servants from contributing any thing at all to this dangerous intimation of idolatry; and that the people might say, Surely those dead men are not so much to be magnified as men mistake, since God will not suffer his holy officers so much as to touch them, not to see them. But those dangers being removed, thou, O my God, dost certainly allow that we should do offices of piety to the dead and that we should draw instructions to piety from the dead. Is not this, O my God, a holy kind of raising up seed to my dead brother, if I, by the meditation of his death produce a better life in myself ? It is the blessing upon Reuben, *Let Reuben live, and not die, and let not his men be few ;*[6] let him propagate many. And it is a malediction, *That that dieth, let it die,*[7] let it do no good in dying; for *trees without fruit,* thou, by thy apostle, callest *twice dead.*[8] It is a second death, if none live the better by me after my death, by the manner of my death. Therefore may I justly think, that thou madest that a way to convey to the Egyptians a fear of thee and a fear of death, that *there was not a house where there was not one dead;*[9] for thereupon the Egyptians said, *We are all dead men:* the death of others should catechise us to death. Thy Son Christ Jesus is the *first begotten of the dead;*[10] he rises first, the eldest brother, and he is my master in this science of death; but yet, for me, I am

[4] Wisd. xiii. 18.   [5] Isaiah, viii. 19.   [6] Deut. xxxiii. 6.
[7] Zech. xi. 9.   [8] Jude, 12.   [9] Exod. xii. 30.
[10] Rev. i. 5.

118

a younger brother too, to this man who died now, and to every man whom I see or hear to die before me, and all they are ushers to me in this school of death. I take therefore that which thy servant David's wife said to him, to be said to me, *If thou save not thy life to-night, to-morrow thou shalt be slain.*[11] If the death of this man work not upon me now, I shall die worse than if thou hadst not afforded me this help; for thou hast sent him in this bell to me, as thou didst send to the angel of Sardis, with commission to *strengthen the things that remain, and that are ready to die,*[12] that in this weakness of body I might receive spiritual strength by these occasions. This is my strength, that whether thou say to me, as thine angel said to Gideon, *Peace be unto thee, fear not, thou shalt not die;*[13] or whether thou say, as unto Aaron, *Thou shalt die there;*[14] yet thou wilt preserve that which is ready to die, my soul, from the worst death, that of sin. Zimri *died for his sins,* says thy Spirit, *which he sinned in doing evil; and in his sin which he did to make Israel sin;*[15] for his sins, his many sins, and then in his sin, his particular sin. For my sins I shall die whensoever I die, for death is the wages of sin; but I shall die in my sin, in that particular sin of resisting thy Spirit, if I apply not thy assistances. Doth it not call us to a particular consideration that thy blessed Son varies his form of commination, and aggravates it in the variation, when he says to the Jews (because they refused the light offered), *You shall die in your sin:*[16] and then when they proceeded to farther disputations, and vexations, and temptations, he adds, *You shall die in your sins ;*[17] he multiplies the former expression to a plural. In this sin,

---

[11] 1 Sam. xix. 11. [12] Rev. iii. 2. [13] Judg. vi. 23.
[14] Numb. xx. 26. [15] 1 Kings, xvi. 19.
[16] John, viii. 21. [17] John, viii. 24.

and in all your sins, doth not the resisting of thy particular helps at last draw upon us the guiltiness of all our former sins? May not the neglecting of this sound ministered to me in this man's death, bring me to that misery, so that I, whom the Lord of life loved so as to die for me, shall die, and a creature of mine own shall be immortal; that I shall die, and the *worm* of mine own conscience *shall never die* ?[18]

XVIII. PRAYER.

O ETERNAL and most gracious God, I have a new occasion of thanks, and a new occasion of prayer to thee from the ringing of this bell. Thou toldest me in the other voice that I was mortal and approaching to death; in this I may hear thee say that I am dead in an irremediable, in an irrecoverable state for bodily health. If that be thy language in this voice, how infinitely am I bound to thy heavenly Majesty for speaking so plainly unto me? for even that voice, that I must die now, is not the voice of a judge that speaks by way of condemnation, but of a physician that presents health in that. Thou presentest me death as the cure of my disease, not as the exaltation of it; if I mistake thy voice herein, if I overrun thy pace, and prevent thy hand, and imagine death more instant upon me than thou hast bid him be, yet the voice belongs to me; I am dead, I was born dead, and from the first laying of these mud walls in my conception, they have mouldered away, and the whole course of life is but an active death. Whether this voice instruct me that I am a dead man now, or remember me that I have been a dead man all this while,

---

[18] Isaiah, lxvi. 24.

I humbly thank thee for speaking in this voice to my soul; and I humbly beseech thee also to accept my prayers in his behalf, by whose occasion this voice, this sound, is come to me. For though he be by death transplanted to thee, and so in possession of inexpressible happiness there, yet here upon earth thou hast given us such a portion of heaven, as that though men dispute whether thy saints in heaven do know what we in earth in particular do stand in need of, yet, without all disputation, we upon earth do know what thy saints in heaven lack yet for the consummation of their happiness, and therefore thou hast afforded us the dignity that we may pray for them. That therefore this soul, now newly departed to thy kingdom, may quickly return to a joyful reunion to that body which it hath left, and that we with it may soon enjoy the full consummation of all in body and soul, I humbly beg at thy hand, O our most merciful God, for thy Son Christ Jesus' sake. That that blessed Son of thine may have the consummation of his dignity, by entering into his last office, the office of a judge, and may have society of human bodies in heaven, as well as he hath had ever of souls; and that as thou hatest sin itself, thy hate to sin may be expressed in the abolishing of all instruments of sin, the allurements of this world, and the world itself; and all the temporary revenges of sin, the stings of sickness and of death; and all the castles, and prisons, and monuments of sin, in the grave. That time may be swallowed up in eternity, and hope swallowed in possession, and ends swallowed in infiniteness, and all men ordained to salvation in body and soul be one entire and everlasting sacrifice to thee, where thou mayst receive delight from them, and they glory from thee, for evermore. Amen.

121

XIX. Oceano tandem emenso, aspicienda resurgit
Terra; vident, justis, medici, jam cocta mederi
Se posse, indiciis.

*At last the physicians, after a long and stormy voyage, see
land: they have so good signs of the concoction of the
disease, as that they may safely proceed to purge.*

XIX. MEDITATION.

ALL this while the physicians themselves have been
patients, patiently attending when they should see
any land in this sea, any earth, any cloud, any
indication of concoction in these waters. Any disorder
of mine, any pretermission of theirs, exalts the disease,
accelerates the rages of it; no diligence accelerates the
concoction, the maturity of the disease; they must
stay till the season of the sickness come; and till it be
ripened of itself, and then they may put to their hand
to gather it before it fall off, but they cannot hasten
the ripening. Why should we look for it in a disease,
which is the disorder, the discord, the irregularity, the
commotion and rebellion of the body? It were scarce
a disease if it could be ordered and made obedient to our
times. Why should we look for that in disorder, in a
disease, when we cannot have it in nature, who is so
regular and so pregnant, so forward to bring her work
to perfection and to light? Yet we cannot awake the
July flowers in January, nor retard the flowers of the
spring to autumn. We cannot bid the fruits come in
May, nor the leaves to stick on in December A woman
that is weak cannot put off her ninth month to a tenth
for her delivery, and say she will stay till she be stronger;
nor a queen cannot hasten it to a seventh, that she may
be ready for some other pleasure. Nature (if we look

for durable and vigorous effects) will not admit preventions, nor anticipations, nor obligations upon her, for they are precontracts, and she will be left to her liberty. Nature would not be spurred, nor forced to mend her pace; nor power, the power of man, greatness, loves not that kind of violence neither. There are of them that will give, that will do justice, that will pardon, but they have their own seasons for all these, and he that knows not them shall starve before that gift come, and ruin before the justice, and die before the pardon save him. Some tree bears no fruit, except much dung be laid about it; and justice comes not from some till they be richly manured: some trees require much visiting, much watering, much labour; and some men give not their fruits but upon importunity: some trees require incision, and pruning, and lopping; some men must be intimidated and syndicated with commissions, before they will deliver the fruits of justice: some trees require the early and the often access of the sun; some men open not, but upon the favours and letters of court mediation: some trees must be housed and kept within doors; some men lock up, not only their liberality, but their justice and their compassion, till the solicitation of a wife, or a son, or a friend, or a servant, turn the key. Reward is the season of one man, and importunity of another; fear the season of one man, and favour of another; friendship the season of one man, and natural affection of another; and he that knows not their seasons, nor cannot stay them, must lose the fruits: as nature will not, so power and greatness will not be put to change their seasons, and shall we look for this indulgence in a disease, or think to shake it off before it be ripe? All this while, therefore, we are but upon a defensive war, and that is but a doubtful state; especially where they who are besieged do know the best of their defences, and do not know the worst of their enemy's power; when they cannot mend their works within, and the enemy can increase his numbers without. O how many far more miserable, and far more worthy to be less miserable than I, are besieged with this sickness, and lack their sentinels, their physicians to watch, and lack their munition, their cordials to defend, and perish before the enemy's weakness might invite them to sally, before the disease show any declination, or admit any way of working upon itself? In me the siege is so far slackened, as that we may come to fight, and so die in the field, if I die, and not in a prison.

XIX. EXPOSTULATION.

MY God, my God, thou art a direct God, may I not say a literal God, a God that wouldst be understood literally and according to the plain sense of all that thou sayest? but thou art also (Lord, I intend it to thy glory, and let no profane misinterpreter abuse it to thy diminution), thou art a figurative, a metaphorical God too; a God in whose words there is such a height of figures, such voyages, such peregrinations to fetch remote and precious metaphors, such extensions, such spreadings, such curtains of allegories, such third heavens of hyperboles, so harmonious elocutions, so retired and so reserved expressions, so commanding persuasions, so persuading commandments, such sinews even in thy milk, and such things in thy words, as all profane authors seem of the seed of the serpent that creeps, thou art the Dove that flies. O, what words but thine can express the inexpressible texture and composition of thy word, in which to one man that argument that binds his faith to believe that to be the word of God, is the reverent simplicity of the word, and to another the majesty of the word; and in which two men equally pious may meet, and one wonder that all should not understand it, and the other as much that any man should. So, Lord, thou givest us the same earth to labour on and to lie in, a house and a grave of the same earth; so, Lord, thou givest us the same word for our satisfaction and for our inquisition, for our instruction and for our admiration too; for there are places that thy servants Hierom and Augustine would scarce believe (when they grew warm by mutual letters) of one another, that they understood them, and yet both Hierom and Augustine call upon persons whom they knew to be far weaker than they thought one another (old women and young maids) to read the Scriptures, without confining them to these or those places. Neither art thou thus a figurative, a metaphorical God in thy word only, but in thy works too. The style of thy works, the phrase of thine actions, is metaphorical The institution of thy whole worship in the old law was a continual allegory; types and figures overspread all, and figures flowed into figures, and poured themselves out into farther figures; circumcision carried a figure of baptism, and baptism carries a figure of that purity which we shall have in perfection in the new Jerusalem. Neither didst thou speak and work in this language only in the time of thy prophets; but since thou spokest in thy Son it is so too. How often, how much more often, doth thy Son call himself a way, and a light, and a gate, and a vine, and bread, than the Son of God, or of man? How much oftener doth he exhibit a metaphorical Christ, than a real, a literal? This hath occasioned thine ancient servants, whose delight it was to write after thy copy, to proceed the same way in their expositions of the Scriptures, and in their composing both of public liturgies and of private prayers to thee, to make their accesses to thee in such a kind of language as thou wast pleased to speak to them, in a figurative, in a metaphorical language, in which manner I am bold to call the comfort which I receive now in this sickness in the indication of the concoction and maturity thereof, in certain clouds and recidences, which the physicians observe, a discovering of land from sea after a long and tempestuous voyage. But wherefore, O my God, hast thou presented to us the afflictions and calamities of this life in the name of waters? so often in the name of waters, and deep waters, and seas of waters? Must we look to be drowned? are they bottomless, are they boundless? That is not the dialect of thy language; thou hast given a remedy against the deepest water by water; against the inundation of sin by baptism; and the first life that thou gavest to any creatures was in waters: therefore thou dost not threaten us with an irremediableness when our affliction is a sea. It is so if we consider ourselves; so thou callest Genezareth, which was but a lake, and not salt, a sea; so thou callest the Mediterranean sea still the great sea, because the inhabitants saw no other sea; they that dwelt there thought a lake a sea, and the others thought a little sea, the greatest, and we that know not the afflictions of others call our own the heaviest. But, O my God, that is truly great that overflows the channel, that is really a great affliction which is above my strength; but thou, O God, art my strength, and then what can be above it? *Mountains shake with the swelling of thy sea;*[1] secular mountains, men strong in power; spiritual mountains, men strong in grace, are shaken with afflictions; but *thou layest up thy sea in storehouses;*[2] even

---

[1] Psalm xlvi. 3.   [2] Psalm xxxiii. 7.

thy corrections are of thy treasure, and thou wilt not waste thy corrections; when they have done their service to humble thy patient, thou wilt call them in again, for *thou givest the sea thy decree, that the waters should not pass thy commandment.*[3] All our waters shall run into Jordan, and thy servants passed Jordan dry foot;[4] they shall run into the red sea (the sea of thy Son's blood), and the red sea, that red sea, drowns none of thine: but *they that sail on the sea tell of the danger thereof.*[5] I that am yet in this affliction, owe thee the glory of speaking of it; but, as the wise man bids me, I say, I *may speak much and come short, wherefore in sum thou art all.*[6] Since thou art so, O my God, and affliction is a sea too deep for us, what is our refuge? Thine ark, thy ship. In all other afflictions, those means which thou hast ordained in this sea, in sickness, thy ship is thy physician. *Thou hast made a way in the sea, and a safe path in the waters, showing that thou canst save from all dangers, yea, though a man went to sea without art:*[7] yet, where I find all that, I find this added; *nevertheless thou wouldst not, that the work of thy wisdom should be idle.*[8] Thou canst save without means, but thou hast told no man that thou wilt; thou hast told every man that thou wilt not.[9] When the centurion believed the master of the ship more than St. Paul, they were all opened to a great danger; this was a preferring of thy means before thee, the author of the means: but, my God, though thou beest every where: I have no promise of appearing to me but in thy ship, thy blessed Son preached out of a ship:[10] the means is preaching, he did that; and the ship was a type of the church, he did it there. Thou gavest St. Paul the lives

---

[3] Prov. viii. 29.   .[4] Josh. iii. 17.   .[5] Ecclus. xliii. 24.
[6] Ecclus. xliii. 27.   .[7] Wisd. xiv. 3.   .[8] Wisd. xiv. 5.
[9] Acts, xxvii. 11.   [10] Luke, v. 3.

of all them that sailed with him;[11] if they had not been in the ship with him, the gift had not extended to them. *As soon as thy Son was come out of the ship, immediately there met him, out of the tombs, a man with an unclean spirit, and no man could hold him, no not with chains.*[12] Thy Son needed no use of means; yet there we apprehend the danger to us, if we leave the ship, the means, in this case the physician. But as they are ships to us in those seas, so is there a ship to them too in which they are to stay. Give me leave, O my God, to assist myself with such a construction of these words of thy servant Paul to the centurion, when the mariners would have left the ship, *Except these abide in the ship, you cannot be safe:*[13] except they who are our ships, the physicians, abide in that which is theirs, and our ship, the truth, and the sincere and religious worship of thee and thy gospel, we cannot promise ourselves so good safety; for though we have our ship, the physician, he hath not his ship, religion; and means are not means but in their concatenation, as they depend and are chained together. *The ships are great,* says thy apostle, *but a helm turns them;*[14] the men are learned, but their religion turns their labours to good, and therefore it was a heavy curse when *the third part of the ships perished:*[15] it is a heavy case where either all religion, or true religion, should forsake many of these ships whom thou hast sent to convey us over these seas. But, O my God, my God, since I have my ship and they theirs, I have them and they have thee, why are we yet no nearer land? As soon as thy Son's disciple had taken him into the ship, *immediately the ship was at the land whither they went.*[16] Why have not they and I this dispatch? Every thing is

---

[11] Acts, xxvii. 24. [12] Mark, v. 2. [13] Acts, xxvii. 31.
[41] James, iii. 4. [15] Rev. viii. 9. [16] John, vi. 21.

immediately done, which is done when thou wouldst have it done. Thy purpose terminates every action, and what was done before that is undone yet. Shall that slacken my hope? thy prophet from thee hath forbidden it. *It is good that a man should both hope, and quietly wait for the salvation of the Lord.*[17] Thou puttest off many judgments till the last day, and many pass this life without any; and shall not I endure the putting off thy mercy for a day? And yet, O my God, thou puttest me not to that, for the assurance of future mercy is present mercy. But what is my assurance now? what is my seal? It is but a cloud; that which my physicians call a cloud, in that which gives them their indication. But a cloud? Thy great seal to all the world, the rainbow, that secured the world for ever from drowning, was but a reflection upon a cloud. A cloud itself was a pillar which guided the church,[18] and the glory of God not only was, but appeared in a cloud.[19] Let me return, O my God, to the consideration of thy servant Elijah's proceeding in a time of desperate drought;[20] he bids them look towards the sea; they look, and see nothing. He bids them again and again seven times; and at the seventh time they saw a little cloud rising out of the sea, and presently they had their desire of rain. Seven days, O my God, have we looked for this cloud, and now we have it; none of thy indications are frivolous, thou makest thy signs seals, and thy seals effects, and thy effects consolation and restitution, wheresoever thou mayst receive glory by that way.

[17] Lam. iii. 26. [18] Exod. xiii. 21. [19] Exod. xvi. 10.
[20] 1 Kings, xviii. 43.

129

IV. PRAYER.

O ETERNAL and most gracious God, who though thou passedst over infinite millions of generations, before thou camest to a creation of this world, yet when thou beganst, didst never intermit that work, but continuedst day to day, till thou hadst perfected all the work, and deposed it in the hands and rest of a sabbath, though thou have been pleased to glorify thyself in a long exercise of my patience, with an expectation of thy declaration of thyself in this my sickness, yet since thou hast now of thy goodness afforded that which affords us some hope, if that be still the way of thy glory, proceed in that way and perfect that work, and establish me in a sabbath and rest in thee, by this thy seal of bodily restitution. Thy priests came up to thee by steps in the temple; thy angels came down to Jacob by steps upon the ladder; we find no stair by which thou thyself camest to Adam in paradise, nor to Sodom in thine anger; for thou, and thou only, art able to do all at once. But O Lord, I am not weary of thy pace, nor weary of mine own patience. I provoke thee not with a prayer, not with a wish, not with a hope, to more haste than consists with thy purpose, nor look that any other thing should have entered into thy purpose, but thy glory. To hear thy steps coming towards me is the same comfort as to see thy face present with me; whether thou do the work of a thousand years in a day, or extend the work of a day to a thousand years, as long as thou workest, it is light and comfort. Heaven itself is but an extension of the same joy; and an extension of this mercy, to proceed at thy leisure, in the way of restitution, is a manifestation of heaven to me here upon earth. From that people to whom thou appearedst in

130

signs and in types, the Jews, thou art departed, because they trusted in them; but from thy church, to whom thou hast appeared in thyself, in thy Son, thou wilt never depart, because we cannot trust too much in him. Though thou have afforded me these signs of restitution, yet if I confide in them, and begin to say, all was but a natural accident, and nature begins to discharge herself, and she will perfect the whole work, my hope shall vanish because it is not in thee. If thou shouldst take thy hand utterly from me, and have nothing to do with me, nature alone were able to destroy me; but if thou withdraw thy helping hand, alas, how frivolous are the helps of nature, how impotent the assistances of art? As therefore the morning dew is a pawn of the evening fatness, so, O Lord, let this day's comfort be the earnest of to-morrow's, so far as may conform me entirely to thee, to what end, and by what way soever thy mercy have appointed me.

XX. Id agunt.

Upon these indications of digested matter, they proceed to purge.

XX. MEDITATION.

THOUGH counsel seem rather to consist of spiritual parts than action, yet action is the spirit and the soul of counsel. Counsels are not always determined in resolutions, we cannot always say, this was concluded; actions are always determined in effects, we can say, this was done. Then have laws their reverence and their majesty, when we see the judge upon the bench executing them. Then have counsels of war their impressions and their operations, when we see the seal of an army set to them. It was an ancient way of celebrating the memory of such as deserved well of the state, to afford them that kind of statuary representation, which was then called Hermes, which was the head and shoulders of a man standing upon a cube, but those shoulders without arms and hands. Altogether it figured a constant supporter of the state, by his counsel; but in this hieroglyphic, which they made without hands, they pass their consideration no farther but that the counsellor should be without hands, so far as not to reach out his hand to foreign temptations of bribes, in matters of counsel, and that it was not necessary that the head should employ his own hand; that the same men should serve in the execution which assisted in the counsel; but that there should not belong hands to every head, action to every counsel, was never intended so much as in figure and representation. For as matrimony is scarce to be called matrimony where there is a resolution against the fruits of matrimony, against the having of children,[1] so counsels are not counsels, but illusions, where there is from the beginning no purpose to execute the determinations of those counsels. The arts and sciences are most properly referred to the head; that is their proper element and sphere; but yet the art of proving, logic, and the art of persuading, rhetoric, are deduced to the hand, and that expressed by a hand contracted into a fist, and this by a hand enlarged and expanded; and evermore the power of man, and the power of God, himself is expressed so. All things are in his hand; neither is God so often presented to us, by names that carry our consideration upon counsel, as upon execution of counsel; he oftener is called the Lord of Hosts than by all other names, that may be

[1] August.

referred to the other signification. Hereby therefore we take into our meditation the slippery condition of man, whose happiness in any kind, the defect of any one thing conducing to that happiness, may ruin; but it must have all the pieces to make it up. Without counsel, I had not got thus far; without action and practice, I should go no farther towards health. But what is the present necessary action? Purging; a withdrawing, a violating of nature, a farther weakening. O dear price, and O strange way of addition, to do it by subtraction; of restoring nature, to violate nature; of providing strength, by increasing weakness. Was I not sick before? And is it a question of comfort to be asked now, did your physic make you sick? Was that it that my physic promised, to make me sick? This is another step upon which we may stand, and see farther into the misery of man, the time, the season of his misery; it must be done now. O over-cunning, over-watchful, over-diligent, and over-sociable misery of man, that seldom comes alone, but then when it may accompany other miseries, and so put one another into the higher exaltation, and better heart. I am ground even to an attenuation and must proceed to evacuation, all ways to exinanition and annihilation.

XX. EXPOSTULATION.

MY God, my God, the God of order, but yet not of ambition, who assignest place to every on , but not contention for place, when shall it be thy pleasure to put an end to all these quarrels for spiritual precedences? When shall men leave their uncharitable disputations, which is to take place, faith or repentance, and which, when we consider faith and works? The head and the hand too are required to a perfect natural man; counsel and action too, to a perfect civil man; faith and works too, to him that is perfectly spiritual   But because it is easily said, I believe, and because it doth not easily lie in proof, nor is easily demonstrable by any evidence taken from my heart (for who sees that, who searches those rolls?) whether I do believe or no, is it not therefore, O my God, that thou dost so frequently, so earnestly, refer us to the hand, to the observation of actions?   There is a little suspicion, a little imputation laid upon over-tedious and dilatory counsels.   Many good occasions slip away in long consultations; and it may be a degree of sloth, to be too long in mending nets, though that must be done. *He that observeth the wind shall not sow, and he that regardeth the clouds shall not reap;*[2] that is, he that is too dilatory, too superstitious in these observations, and studies but the excuse of his own idleness in them; but that which the same wise and royal servant of thine says in another place, all accept, and ask no comment upon it, *He becometh poor that dealeth with a slack hand, but the hand of the diligent maketh rich;*[3] all evil imputed to the absence, all good attributed to the presence of the hand.   I know, my God (and I bless thy name for knowing it, for all good knowledge is from thee), that thou considerest the heart; but thou takest not off thine eye till thou come to the hand.   Nay, my God, doth not thy Spirit intimate that thou beginnest where we begin (at least, hat thou allowest us to begin there), when thou orde est thine own answer to thine own question, *Who shall ascend into the hill of the Lord?* thus, *He that hath clean hands, and a pure heart?*[4]   Dost thou not (at least) send us first to the hand?   And is not the work of their hands that declaration of their holy zeal,

[2] Eccles xi. 4.   [3] Prov. x. 4.   [4] Psalm xxiv. 3.

in the present execution of manifest idolators, called a consecration of themselves,[5] by thy Holy Spirit? Their hands are called all themselves; for even counsel itself goes under that name in thy word, who knowest best how to give right names: because the counsel of the priests assisted David,[6] Saul says the hand of the priest is with David. And that which is often said by Moses, is very often repeated by thy other prophets, *These and these things the Lord spake,*[7] and *the Lord said,* and *the Lord commanded,* not by the counsels, not by the voice, but by the *hand of Moses,* and by the *hand of the prophets.* Evermore we are referred for our evidence of others, and of ourselves, to the hand, to action, to works. There is something before it, believing; and there is something after it, suffering; but in the most eminent, and obvious, and conspicuous place stands doing. Why then, O my God, my blessed God, in the ways of my spiritual strength, come I so slow to action? I was whipped by thy rod, before I came to consultation, to consider my state; and shall I go no farther? As he that would describe a circle in paper, if he have brought that circle within one inch of finishing, yet if he remove his compass he cannot make it up a perfect circle except he fall to work again, to find out the same centre, so, though setting that foot of my compass upon thee, I have gone so far as to the consideration of myself, yet if I depart from thee, my centre, all is imperfect. This proceeding to action, therefore, is a returning to thee, and a working upon myself by thy physic, by thy purgative physic, a free and entire evacuation of my soul by confession. The working of purgative physic is violent and contrary to nature. O Lord, I decline not this potion of confession, however it may be contrary to a natural man. To take

[5] Exod. xxxii. 29.   [6] 1 Sam. xxii. 17.   [7] Lev. viii. 36.

135

physic, and not according to the right method, is dangerous.[8]   O Lord, I decline not that method in this physic, in things that burthen my conscience, to make my confession to him, into whose hands thou hast put the power of absolution.   I know that " physic may be made so pleasant as that it may easily be taken; but not so pleasant as the virtue and nature of the medicine be extinguished."[9]   I know I am not submitted to such a confession as is a rack and torture of the conscience; but I know I am not exempt from all.   If it were merely problematical, left merely indifferent whether we should take this physic, use this confession, or no, a great physician acknowledges this to have been his practice, to minister to many things which he was not sure would do good, but never any other thing but such as he was sure would do no harm.[10]   The use of this spiritual physic can certainly do no harm; and the church hath always thought that it might, and, doubtless, many humble souls have found, that it hath done them good. *I will therefore take the cup of salvation, and call upon thy name*[11].   I will find this cup of compunction as full as I have formerly filled the cups of worldly confections, that so I may escape the cup of malediction and irrecoverable destruction that depends upon that.   And since thy blessed and glorious Son, being offered, in the way to his execution, a cup of stupefaction,[12] to take away the sense of his pain (a charity afforded to condemned persons ordinarily in those places and times), refused that ease, and embraced the whole torment, I take not this cup, but this vessel of mine own sins into my contemplation, and I pour them out here according to the motions of thy Holy Spirit, and any where according to the ordinances of thy holy church.

---

[8],[9],[10] Galen.   [11] Psalm cxvi. 13.   [12] Mark, xv. 23.

XX. PRAYER.

O ETERNAL and most gracious God, who having married man and woman together, and made them one flesh, wouldst have them also to become one soul, so as that they might maintain a sympathy in their affections, and have a conformity to one another in the accidents of this world, good or bad; so having married this soul and this body in me, I humbly beseech thee that my soul may look and make her use of thy merciful proceedings towards my bodily restitution, and go the same way to a spiritual. I am come, by thy goodness, to the use of thine ordinary means for my body, to wash away those peccant humours that endangered it. I have, O Lord, a river in my body, but a sea in my soul, and a sea swollen into the depth of a deluge, above the sea. Thou hast raised up certain hills in me heretofore, by which I might have stood safe from these inundations of sin. Even our natural faculties are a hill, and might preserve us from some sin. Education, study, observation, example, are hills too, and might preserve us from some. Thy church, and thy word, and thy sacraments, and thine ordinances are hills above these; thy spirit of remorse, and compunction, and repentance for former sin, are hills too; and to the top of all these hills thou hast brought me heretofore; but this deluge, this inundation, is got above all my hills; and I have sinned and sinned, and multiplied sin to sin, after all these thy assistances against sin, and where is there water enough to wash away this deluge? There is a red sea, greater than this ocean, and there is a little spring, through which this ocean may pour itself into that red sea. Let thy spirit of true contrition and sorrow pass all my sins,

137

through these eyes, into the wounds of thy Son, and I shall be clean, and my soul so much better purged than my body, as it is ordained for better and a longer life.

XXI. ——————————————— ATQUE ANNUIT ILLE,
QUI, PER EOS, CLAMAT, LINQUAS JAM, LAZARE, LECTUM.

God prospers their practice, and he, by them, calls Lazarus out of his tomb, me out of my bed.

XXI. MEDITATION.

IF man had been left alone in this world at first, shall I think that he would not have fallen? If there had been no woman, would not man have served to have been his own tempter? When I see him now subject to infinite weaknesses, fall into infinite sin without any foreign temptations, shall I think he would have had none, if he had been alone? God saw that man needed a helper, if he should be well; but to make woman ill, the devil saw that there needed no third. When God and we were alone in Adam, that was not enough; when the devil and we were alone in Eve, it was enough. O what a giant is man when he fights against himself, and what a dwarf when he needs or exercises his own assistance for himself? I cannot rise out of my bed till the physician enable me, nay, I cannot tell that I am able to rise till he tell me so. I do nothing, I know nothing of myself; how little and how impotent a piece of the world is any man alone? And how much less a piece of himself is that man? So little as that when it falls out (as it falls out in some cases) that more misery and more oppression would be an ease to a man, he cannot give himself that miserable addition of more misery. A man that is pressed to death, and might be eased by more weights, cannot lay those more weights upon himself: he can sin alone, and suffer alone, but not repent, not be absolved, without another. Another tells me, I may rise; and I do so. But is every raising a preferment? or is every present preferment a station? I am readier to fall to the earth, now I am up, than I was when I lay in the bed. O perverse way, irregular motion of man; even rising itself is the way to ruin! How many men are raised, and then do not fill the place they are raised to? No corner of any place can be empty; there can be no vacuity. If that man do not fill the place, other men will; complaints of his insufficiency will fill it; nay, such an abhorring is there in nature of vacuity, that if there be but an imagination of not filling, in any man, that which is but imagination, neither will fill it, that is, rumour and voice, and it will be given out (upon no ground but imagination, and no man knows whose imagination), that he is corrupt in his place, or insufficient in his place, and another prepared to succeed him in his place. A man rises sometimes and stands not, because he doth not or is not believed to fill his place; and sometimes he stands not because he overfills his place. He may bring so much virtue, so much justice, so much integrity to the place, as shall spoil the place, burthen the place; his integrity may be a libel upon his predecessor and cast an infamy upon him, and a burthen upon his successor to proceed by example, and to bring the place itself to an undervalue and the market to an uncertainty. I am up, and I seem to stand, and I go round, and I am a new argument of the new philosophy, that the earth moves round; why may I not believe that the whole earth moves, in a round motion, though that seem to me to stand, when as I seem to stand to my company, and yet am carried in a giddy and circular motion as I stand? Man hath no centre but misery; there, and only there, he is fixed, and sure to find himself. How little soever he be raised, he moves, and moves in a circle giddily; and as in the heavens there are but a few circles that go about the whole world, but many epicycles, and other lesser circles, but yet circles; so of those men which are raised and put into circles, few of them move from place to place, and pass through many and beneficial places, but fall into little circles, and, within a step or two, are at their end, and not so well as they were in the centre, from which they were raised. Every thing serves to exemplify, to illustrate man's misery. But I need go no farther than myself: for a long time I was not able to rise; at last I must be raised by others; and now I am up, I am ready to sink lower than before.

XXI. EXPOSTULATION.

MY God, my God, how large a glass of the next world is this! As we have an art, to cast from one glass to another, and so to carry the species a great way off, so hast thou, that way, much more; we shall have a resurrection in heaven; the knowledge of that thou castest by another glass upon us here; we feel that we have a resurrection from sin, and that by another glass too; we see we have a resurrection of the body from the miseries and calamities of this life. This resurrection of my body shows me the resurrection of my soul; and both here severally, of both together hereafter. Since thy martyrs under the altar press thee with their solicitation for the resurrection of the body to glory, thou wouldst pardon me, if I should press thee by prayer for the accomplishing of this resurrection, which thou hast begun in me, to health. But, O my God, I do not ask, where I might ask amiss, nor beg that which perchance might be worse for me. I have a bed of sin; delight in sin is a bed: I have a grave of sin; senselessness of sin is a grave: and where Lazarus had been four days, I have been fifty years in this putrefaction; why dost thou not call me, as thou didst him, *with a loud voice*,[1] since my soul is as dead as his body was? I need thy thunder, O my God; thy music will not serve me. Thou hast called thy servants, who are to work upon us in thine ordinance, by all these loud names—winds, and chariots, and falls of waters; where thou wouldst be heard, thou wilt be heard. When thy Son concurred with thee to the making of man, there it is but a speaking, but a saying. There, O blessed and glorious Trinity, was none to hear but you three, and you easily hear one another, because you say the same things. But when thy Son came to the work of redemption, thou spokest,[2] and they that heard it took it for thunder; and thy Son himself cried with a loud voice upon the cross twice,[3] as he who was to prepare his coming, John Baptist, was the voice of a crier, and not of a whisperer. Still, if it be thy voice, it is a loud voice. *These words*, says thy Moses, *thou spokest with a great voice, and thou addedst no more*,[4] says he there. That which thou hast said is evident, and it is evident that none can speak so loud; none can bind us to hear him, as we must thee. *The Most High uttered his voice.* What was his voice? *The Lord thundered from heaven*,[5] it might be heard; but this voice, thy voice, is also a *mighty voice*;[6] not only mighty in power, it may be heard, nor mighty in obligation, it should be heard; but mighty in

---

[1] John, xi. 43.   [2] John, xii. 28.   [3] Matt. xxvii. 46, 50.
[4] Deut. v. 22.   [5] 2 Sam. xxii. 14.   [6] Psalm lxviii. 33.

operation, it will be heard; and therefore hast thou bestowed a whole psalm[7] upon us, to lead us to the consideration of thy voice. It is such a voice as that thy Son says, *the dead shall hear it;*[8] and that is my state. And why, O God, dost thou not speak to me, in that effectual loudness? Saint John heard a voice, and *he turned about to see the voice:*[9] sometimes we are too curious of the instrument by what man God speaks; but thou speakest loudest when thou speakest to the heart. *There was silence, and I heard a voice*, says one, to thy servant Job.[10] I hearken after thy voice in thine ordinances, and I seek not a whispering in conventicles; but yet, O my God, speak louder, that so, though I do hear thee now, then I may hear nothing but thee. My sins cry aloud; Cain's murder did so: my afflictions cry aloud; *the floods have lifted up their voice* (and waters are afflictions), *but thou, O Lord, art mightier than the voice of many waters;*[11] than many temporal, many spiritual afflictions, than any of either kind: and why dost thou not speak to me in that voice? *What is man, and whereto serveth he? What is his good and what is his evil?*[12] My bed of sin is not evil, not desperately evil, for thou dost call me out of it; but my rising out of it is not good (not perfectly good), if thou call not·louder, and hold me now I am up. O my God, I am afraid of a fearful application of those words, *When a man hath done, then he beginneth;*[13] when this body is unable to sin, his sinful memory sins over his old sins again; and that which thou wouldst have us to remember for compunction, we remember with delight. *Bring him to me in his bed, that I may kill him,*[14] says Saul of David: thou hast not said so, that is not thy voice.

---

[7] Psalm xxix.   [8] John, v. 25.   [9] Rev. i. 12.
[10] Job, iv. 16.   [11] Psalm xciii. 3, 4.   [12] Ecclus. xviii, 8.
[13] Ecclus. v. 7.   [14] 1 Sam. xix. 15.

Joash's own servants slew him when he was sick in his bed:[15] thou hast not suffered that, that my servants should so much as neglect me, or be weary of me in my sickness. Thou threatenest, that *as a shepherd takes out of the mouth of the lion two legs, or a piece of an ear, so shall the children of Israel, that dwell in Samaria, in the corner of a bed, and in Damascus, in a couch, be taken away;*[16] and even they that are secure from danger shall perish. How much more might I, who was in the bed of death, die? But thou hast not so dealt with me. As they brought out sick persons in beds, that thy servant Peter's shadow might over-shadow them,[17] thou hast, O my God, over-shadowed me, refreshed me; but when wilt thou do more? When wilt thou do all? When wilt thou speak in thy loud voice? When wilt thou bid me *take up my bed and walk* ?[18] As my bed is my affections, when shall I bear them so as to subdue them? As my bed is my afflictions, when shall I bear them so as not to murmur at them? When shall I take up my bed and walk? Not lie down upon it, as it is my pleasure, not sink under it, as it is my correction? But O my God, my God, the God of all flesh, and of all spirit, to let me be content with that in my fainting spirit, which thou declarest in this decayed flesh, that as this body is content to sit still, that it may learn to stand, and to learn by standing to walk, and by walking to travel, so my soul, by obeying this thy voice of rising, may by a farther and farther growth of thy grace proceed so, and be so established, as may remove all suspicions, all jealousies between thee and me, and may speak and hear in such a voice, as that still I may be acceptable to thee, and satisfied from thee.

[15] 2 Chron. xxiv. 25. [16] Amos, iii. 12. [17] Acts, v. 15.
[18] Matt, ix. 6.

XXI. PRAYER.

O ETERNAL and most gracious God, who hast made little things to signify great, and conveyed the infinite merits of thy Son in the water of baptism, and in the bread and wine of thy other sacrament, unto us, receive the sacrifice of my humble thanks, that thou hast not only afforded me the ability to rise out of this bed of weariness and discomfort, but hast also made this bodily rising, by thy grace, an earnest of a second resurrection from sin, and of a third, to everlasting glory. Thy Son himself, always infinite in himself, and incapable of addition, was yet pleased to grow in the Virgin's womb, and to grow in stature in the sight of men. Thy good purposes upon me, I know, have their determination and perfection in thy holy will upon me; there thy grace is, and there I am altogether; but manifest them so unto me, in thy seasons, and in thy measures and degrees, that I may not only have that comfort of knowing thee to be infinitely good, but that also of finding thee to be every day better and better to me; and that as thou gavest Saint Paul the messenger of Satan, to humble him so for my humiliation, thou mayst give me thyself in this knowledge, that what grace soever thou afford me to-day, yet I should perish to-morrow if I had not had to-morrow's grace too. Therefore I beg of thee my daily bread; and as thou gavest me the bread of sorrow for many days, and since the bread of hope for some, and this day the bread of possessing, in rising by that strength, which thou the God of all strength hast infused into me, so, O Lord, continue to me the bread of life: the spiritual bread of life, in a faithful assurance in thee; the sacramental bread of life, in a worthy receiving of thee; and the more real bread of life in an everlasting union to thee. I know, O Lord, that when thou hast created angels, and they saw thee produce fowl, and fish, and beasts, and worms, they did not importune thee, and say, Shall we have no better creatures than these, no better companions than these? but stayed thy leisure, and then had man delivered over to them, not much inferior in nature to themselves. No more do I, O God, now that by thy first mercy I am able to rise, importune thee for present confirmation of health; nor now, that by thy mercy I am brought to see that thy correction hath wrought medicinally upon me, presume I upon that spiritual strength I have; but as I acknowledge that my bodily strength is subject to every puff of wind, so is my spiritual strength to every blast of vanity. Keep me therefore still, O my gracious God, in such a proportion of both strengths, as I may still have something to thank thee for, which I have received, and still something to pray for and ask at thy hand.

XXII. Sᴉᴛ ᴍᴏʀʙɪ ꜰᴏᴍᴇꜱ ᴛɪʙɪ ᴄᴜʀᴀ.

The physicians consider the root and occasion, the embers, and coals, and fuel of the disease, and seek to purge or correct that.

XXII. MEDITATION.

HOW ruinous a farm hath man taken, in taking himself! How ready is the house every day to fall down, and how is all the ground overspread with weeds, all the body with diseases; where not only every turf, but every stone bears weeds; not only every muscle of the flesh, but every bone of the body hath some infirmity; every little flint upon the face of this soil hath some infectious weed, every tooth in our head such a pain as a constant man is afraid of, and yet ashamed of that fear, of that sense of the pain. How dear, and how often a rent doth man pay for his farm! He pays twice a day, in double meals, and how little time he hath to raise his rent! How many holidays to call him from his labour! Every day is half holiday, half spent in sleep. What reparations, and subsidies, and contributions he is put to, besides his rent! What medicines besides his diet; and what inmates he is fain to take in, besides his own family; what infectious diseases from other men! Adam might have had Paradise for dressing and keeping it; and then his rent was not improved to such a labour as would have made his brow sweat; and yet he gave it over; how far greater a rent do we pay for this farm, this body, who pay ourselves, who pay the farm itself, and cannot live upon it! Neither is our labour at an end when we have cut down some weed as soon as it sprung up, corrected some violent and dangerous accident of a disease which would have destroyed speedily, nor when we have pulled up that weed from the very root, recovered entirely and soundly from that particular disease; but the whole ground is of an ill nature, the whole soil ill disposed ; there are inclinations, there is a propenseness to diseases in the body, out of which, without any other disorder, diseases will grow, and so we are put to a continual labour upon this farm, to a continual study of the whole complexion and constitution of our body. In the distempers and diseases of soils, sourness, dryness, weeping, any kind of barrenness, the remedy and the physic is, for a great part, sometimes in themselves; sometimes the very situation relieves them; the hanger of a hill will purge and vent his own malignant moisture, and the burning of the upper turf of some ground (as health from cauterizing) puts a new and a vigorous youth into that soil, and there rises a kind of phœnix out of the ashes, a fruitfulness out of that which was barren before, and by that which is the barrenest of all, ashes. And where the ground cannot give itself physic, yet it receives physic from other grounds, from other soils, which are not the worse for having contributed that help to them from marl in other hills, or from slimy sand in other shores, grounds help themselves, or hurt not other grounds from whence they receive help. But I have taken a farm at this hard rent, and upon those heavy covenants, that it can afford itself no help (no part of my body, if it were cut off, would cure another part; in some cases it might preserve a sound part, but in no case recover an infected); and if my body may have had any physic, any medicine from another body, one man from the flesh of another man (as by mummy, or any such composition), it must be from a man that is dead, and not as in other soils, which are never the worse for contributing their marl or their fat slime to my ground. There is nothing in the same man to help man, nothing in mankind to help one another (in this sort, by way of physic), but that he who ministers the help is in as ill case as he that receives it would have been if he had not had it; for he from whose body the physic comes is dead. When therefore I took this farm, undertook this body, I undertook to drain not a marsh but a moat, where there was, not water mingled to offend, but all was water; I undertook to perfume dung, where no one part but all was equally unsavoury; I undertook to make such a thing wholesome, as was not poison by any manifest quality, intense heat or cold, but poison in the whole substance, and in the specific form of it. To cure the sharp accidents of diseases is a great work; to cure the disease itself is a greater; but to cure the body, the root, the occasion of diseases, is a work reserved for the great physician, which he doth never any other way but by glorifying these bodies in the next world.

XXII. EXPOSTULATION.

MY God, my God, what am I put to when I am put to consider and put off the root, the fuel, the occasion of my sickness? What Hippocrates, what Galen, could show me that in my body? It lies deeper than so, it lies in my soul; and deeper than so, for we may well consider the body before the soul came, before inanimation, to be without sin; and the soul, before it come to the body, before that infection, to be without sin: sin is the root and the fuel of all sickness, and yet that which destroys body and soul is in neither, but in both together. It is the union of the body and soul, and, O my God, could I prevent that, or can I dissolve that? The root and the fuel of my sickness is my sin, my actual sin; but even that sin hath another root, another fuel, original sin; and can I divest that? Wilt thou bid me to separate the leaven that a lump of dough hath received, or the salt, that the water hath contracted, from the sea? Dost thou look, that I should so look to the fuel or embers of sin, that I never take fire? The whole world is a pile of fagots, upon which we are laid, and (as though there were no other) we are the bellows. Ignorance blows the fire. He that touched any unclean thing, though he knew it not, became unclean,[1] and a sacrifice was required (therefore a sin imputed), though it were done in ignorance.[2] Ignorance blows this coal; but then knowledge much more; for there are that *know thy judgments,*

[1] Lev. v. 2.   [2] Num. xv. 24.

*and yet not only do, but have pleasure in others that do
against them.*[3] Nature blows this coal; *by nature we are
the children of wrath;*[4] and the law blows it; thy apostle
Saint Paul found that *sin took occasion by the law,* that
therefore, because it is forbidden, we do some things. If
we break the law, we sin; *sin is the transgression of the
law;*[5] and sin itself becomes a law in our members.[6] Our
fathers have imprinted the seed, infused a spring of sin
in us. *As a fountain casteth out her waters,* we *cast out
our wickedness,* but *we have done worse than our fathers,*[7]
We are open to infinite temptations, and yet, as though
we lacked, we are tempted of our own lusts.[8] And not
satisfied with that, as though we were not powerful
enough, or cunning enough, to demolish or undermine
ourselves, when we ourselves have no pleasure in the sin,
we sin for others' sakes. When Adam sinned for Eve's
sake,[9] and Solomon to gratify his wives,[10] it was an
uxorious sin; when the judges sinned for Jezebel's sake,[11]
and Joab to obey David,[12] it was an ambitious sin; when
Pilate sinned to humour the people,[13] and Herod to give
farther contentment to the Jews,[14] it was a popular sin.
Any thing serves to occasion sin, at home in my bosom,
or abroad in my mark and aim; that which I am, and
that which I am not, that which I would be, proves coals,
and embers, and fuel, and bellows to sin; and dost thou
put me, O my God, to discharge myself of myself, before
I can be well? When thou bidst me *to put off the old
man,*[15] dost thou mean not only my old habits of actual
sin, but the oldest of all, original sin? When thou bidst
me *purge out the leaven,*[16] dost thou mean not only the

[3] Rom. i. 32.　　　　[4] Eph. ii. 3.　　　　[5] 1 John, iii. 4.
[6] Rom. vii. 23.　　　[7] Jer. vi. 7; vii. 26.　[8] James, i. 14.
[9] Gen. iii. 6.　　　　[10] 1 Kings, xi. 3.　　[11] 1 Kings, xxi.
[12] 2 Sam. xi. 16—21.　[13] Luke, xxiii. 23.　[14] Acts, xii. 3.
[15] Eph. iv. 22.　　　　[16] 1 Cor. v. 7.

sourness of mine own ill contracted customs, but the innate tincture of sin imprinted by nature? How shall I do that which thou requirest, and not falsify that which thou hast said, that sin is gone over all? But, O my God, I press thee not with thine own text, without thine own comment; I know that in the state of my body, which is more discernible than that of my soul, thou dost effigiate my soul to me. And though no anatomist can say, in dissecting a body, " Here lay the coal, the fuel, the occasion of all bodily diseases," but yet a man may have such a knowledge of his own constitution and bodily inclination to diseases, as that he may prevent his danger in a great part; so, though we cannot assign the place of original sin, nor the nature of it, so exactly as of actual, or by any diligence divest it, yet, having washed it in the water of thy baptism, we have not only so cleansed it, that we may the better look upon it and discern it, but so weakened it, that howsoever it may retain the former nature, it doth not retain the former force, and though it may have the same name, it hath not the same venom.

XXII. PRAYER.

O ETERNAL and most gracious God, the God of security, and the enemy of security too, who wouldst have us always sure of thy love, and yet wouldst have us always doing something for it, let me always so apprehend thee as present with me, and yet so follow after thee, as though I had not apprehended thee. Thou enlargedst Hezekiah's lease for fifteen years; thou renewedst Lazarus's lease for a time which we know not; but thou didst never so put out any of these fires as that thou didst not rake up the embers, and

150

wrap up a future mortality in that body, which thou hadst then so reprieved. Thou proceedest no otherwise in our souls, O our good but fearful God; thou pardonest no sin, so as that that sinner can sin no more; thou makest no man so acceptable as that thou makest him impeccable. Though therefore it were a diminution of the largeness, and derogatory to the fulness of thy mercy, to look back upon the sins which in a true repentance I have buried in the wounds of thy Son, with a jealous or suspicious eye, as though they were now my sins, when I had so transferred them upon thy Son, as though they could now be raised to life again, to condemn me to death, when they are dead in him who is the fountain of life, yet were it an irregular anticipation, and an insolent presumption, to think that thy present mercy extended to all my future sins, or that there were no embers, no coals, of future sins left in me. Temper therefore thy mercy so to my soul, O my God, that I may neither decline to any faintness of spirit, in suspecting thy mercy now to be less hearty, less sincere, than it uses to be, to those who are perfectly reconciled to thee, nor presume so of it as either to think this present mercy an antidote against all poisons, and so expose myself to temptations, upon confidence that this thy mercy shall preserve me, or that when I do cast myself into new sins, I may have new mercy at any time, because thou didst so easily afford me this.

XXIII. METUSQUE, RELABI.

They warn me of the fearful danger of relapsing.

XXIII. MEDITATION.

IT is not in man's body, as it is in the city, that when the bell hath rung, to cover your fire, and rake up the embers, you may lie down and sleep without fear. Though you have by physic and diet raked up the embers of your disease, still there is a fear of a relapse; and the greater danger is in that. Even in pleasures and in pains, there is a proprietary, a *meum et tuum*, and a man is most affected with that pleasure which is his, his by former enjoying and experience, and most intimidated with those pains which are his, his by a woful sense of them, in former afflictions. A covetous person, who hath preoccupated all his senses, filled all his capacities with the delight of gathering, wonders how any man can have any taste of any pleasure in any openness or liberality; so also in bodily pains, in a fit of the stone, the patient wonders why any man should call the gout a pain; and he that hath felt neither, but the toothache, is as much afraid of a fit of that as either of the other of either of the other. Diseases which we never felt in ourselves come but to a compassion of others that have endured them; nay, compassion itself comes to no great degree if we have not felt in some proportion in ourselves that which we lament and condole in another. But when we have had those torments in their exaltation ourselves, we tremble at relapse. When we must pant through all those fiery heats, and sail through all those overflowing sweats, when we must watch through all those long nights, and mourn through all those long days (days and nights, so long as that Nature herself shall seem to be perverted, and to have put the longest day, and the longest night, which should be six months asunder, into one natural, unnatural day), when we must stand at the same bar, expect the return of physicians from their consultations, and not be sure of the same verdict, in any good indications, when we must go the same way over again, and not see the same issue, that is a state, a condition, a calamity, in respect of which any other sickness were a convalescence, and any greater, less. It adds to the affliction, that relapses are (and for the most part justly) imputed to ourselves, as occasioned by some disorder in us; and so we are not only passive but active in our own ruin; we do not only stand under a falling house, but pull it down upon us; and we are not only executed (that implies guiltiness), but we are executioners (that implies dishonour), and executioners of ourselves (and that implies impiety). And we fall from that comfort which we might have in our first sickness, from that meditation, " Alas, how generally miserable is man, and how subject to diseases " (for in that it is some degree of comfort that we are but in the state common to all), we fall, I say, to this discomfort, and self-accusing, and self-condemning: " Alas, how improvident, and in that how unthankful to God and his instruments, am I in making so ill use of so great benefits, in destroying so soon so long a work, in relapsing, by my disorder, to that from which they had delivered me ": and so my meditation is fearfully transferred from the body to the mind, and from the consideration of the sickness to that sin, that sinful carelessness, by which I have occasioned my relapse. And amongst the many weights that aggravate a relapse, this also is one, that a relapse proceeds with a more violent dispatch, and more irremediably, because it finds the country weakened, and depopulated before.

153

Upon a sickness, which as yet appears not, we can scarce fix a fear, because we know not what to fear; but as fear is the busiest and irksomest affection, so is a relapse (which is still ready to come) into that which is but newly gone, the nearest object, the most immediate exercise of that affection of fear.

XXIII. EXPOSTULATION.

MY God, my God, my God, thou mighty Father, who hast been my physician; thou glorious Son, who hast been my physic; thou blessed Spirit, who hast prepared and applied all to me, shall I alone be able to overthrow the work of all you, and relapse into those spiritual sicknesses from which infinite mercies have withdrawn me? Though thou, O my God, have filled my measure with mercy, yet my measure was not so large as that of thy whole people, the nation, the numerous and glorious nation of Israel; and yet how often, how often did they fall into relapses! And then, where is my assurance? How easily thou passedst over many other sins in them, and how vehemently thou insistedst in those into which they so often relapsed; those were their murmurings against thee, in thine instruments and ministers, and their turnings upon other gods, and embracing the idolatries of their neighbours. O my God, how slippery a way, to how irrecoverable a bottom, is murmuring; and how near thyself he comes, that murmurs at him who comes from thee! The magistrate is the garment in which thou apparelest thyself, and he that shoots at the clothes cannot say he meant no ill to the man: thy people were fearful examples of that, for how often did their murmuring against thy ministers end in a departing from thee! When they would have other officers, they would have other gods; and still to-day's murmuring was to-morrow's idolatry; as their murmuring induced idolatry, and they relapsed often into both, I have found in myself, O my God (O my God, thou hast found it in me, and thy finding it hast showed it to me) such a transmigration of sin, as makes me afraid of relapsing too. The soul of sin (for we have made sin immortal, and it must have a soul), the soul of sin is disobedience to thee; and when one sin hath been dead in me, that soul hath passed into another sin. Our youth dies, and the sins of our youth with it; some sins die a violent death, and some a natural; poverty, penury, imprisonment, banishment, kill some sins in us, and some die of age; many ways we become unable to do that sin, but still the soul lives and passes into another sin; and that that was licentiousness grows ambition, and that comes to indevotion and spiritual coldness: we have three lives in our state of sin, and where the sins of youth expire, those of our middle years enter, and those of our age after them. This transmigration of sin found in myself, makes me afraid, O my God, of a relapse; but the occasion of my fear is more pregnant than so, for I have had, I have multiplied relapses already. Why, O my God, is a relapse so odious to thee? Not so much their murmuring and their idolatry, as their relapsing into those sins, seems to affect thee in thy disobedient people. *They limited the holy One of Israel,*[1] as thou complainest of them: that was a murmuring; but before thou chargest them with the fault itself, in the same place thou chargest them with the iterating, the redoubling of that fault before the fault was named; *How oft did they provoke me in the wilderness, and grieve me in the desert?* That which brings thee to

[1] Psalm lxxviii. 41.

that exasperation against them, as to say, that thou wouldst break thine own oath rather than leave them unpunished (*They shall not see the land which I sware unto their fathers*) was because *they had tempted thee ten times*,[2] infinitely; upon that thou threatenest with that vehemency, *If you do in any wise go back, know for a certainty God will no more drive out any of these nations from before you; but they shall be snares and traps unto you, and scourges in your sides, and thorns in your eyes, till ye perish.*[3] No tongue but thine own, O my God, can express thine indignation against a nation relapsing to idolatry. Idolatry in any nation is deadly, but when the disease is complicated with a relapse (a knowledge and a profession of a former recovery), it is desperate; and thine anger works, not only where the evidence is pregnant and without exception (so thou sayest when it is said, that certain men in a city have withdrawn others to idolatry, and that inquiry is made, and it is found true; the city, and the inhabitants, and the cattle are to be destroyed),[4] but where there is but a suspicion, a rumour, of such a relapse to idolatry, thine anger is awakened, and thine indignation stirred. In the government of thy servant Joshua, there was a voice, that Reuben and Gad, with those of Manasseh, had built a new altar.[5] Israel doth not send one to inquire, but the whole congregation gathered to go up to war against them,[6] and there went a prince of every tribe; and they object to them, not so much their present declination to idolatry, as their relapse: *Is the iniquity of Peor too little for us?*[7] an idolatry formerly committed, and punished with the slaughter of twenty-four thousand delinquents. At last Reuben and Gad satisfy them, that that altar was not built for idolatry, but built as a pattern of theirs, that

[2] Numb. xiv. 22, 23. [3] Josh. xxiii. 12, 13. [4] Deut. xiii. 12-16.
[5] [6] Josh. xxii. 11, 12. [7] Josh. xxii. 17.

they might thereby profess themselves to be of the same profession that they were, and so the army returned without blood. Even where it comes not so far as to an actual relapse into idolatry, thou, O my God, becomest sensible of it; though thou, who seest the heart all the way, preventest all dangerous effects where there was no ill meaning, however there were occasion of suspicious rumours given to thine Israel of relapsing. So odious to thee, and so aggravating a weight upon sin is a relapse. But, O my God, why is it so? so odious? It must be so, because he that hath sinned and then repented, hath weighed God and the devil in a balance; he hath heard God and the devil plead, and after hearing given judgment on that side to which he adheres by his subsequent practice;[8] if he return to his sin, he decrees for Satan, he prefers sin before grace, and Satan before God; and in contempt of God, declares the precedency for his adversary; and a contempt wounds deeper than an injury, a relapse deeper than a blasphemy. And when thou hast told me that a relapse is more odious to thee, need I ask why it is more dangerous, more pernicious to me? Is there any other measure of the greatness of my danger, than the greatness of thy displeasure? How fitly and how fearfully hast thou expressed my case in a storm at sea, if I relapse; *They mount up to heaven, and they go down again to the depth!*[9] My sickness brought me to thee in repentance, and my relapse hath cast me farther from thee. *The end of that man shall be worse than the beginning,*[10] says thy Word, thy Son; my beginning was sickness, punishment for sin: but *a worse thing may follow,*[11] says he also, if I sin again; not only death, which is an end worse than sickness, which was the beginning, but hell, which

---

[8] Tertullian. [9] Psalm cvii. 26.
[10] Matt. xii. 45. [11] John, v. 14.

is a beginning worse than that end. Thy great servant denied thy Son,[12] and he denied him again, but all before repentance; here was no relapse. O, if thou hadst ever readmitted Adam into Paradise, how abstinently would he have walked by that tree! And would not the angels that fell have fixed themselves upon thee, if thou hadst once readmitted them to thy sight? They never relapsed; if I do, must not my case be as desperate ? Not so desperate; for *as thy majesty, so is thy mercy*,[13] both infinite; and thou, who hast commanded me to pardon my brother seventy-seven times, hast limited thyself to no number. If death were ill in itself, thou wouldst never have raised any dead man to life again, because that man must necessarily die again. If thy mercy in pardoning did so far aggravate a relapse, as that there were no more mercy after it, our case were the worse for that former mercy; for who is not under even a necessity of sinning whilst he is here, if we place this necessity in our own infirmity, and not in thy decree? But I speak not this, O my God, as preparing a way to my relapse out of presumption, but to preclude all accesses of desperation, though out of infirmity I should relapse.

XXIII. PRAYER.

O ETERNAL and most gracious God, who, though thou beest ever infinite, yet enlargest thyself by the number of our prayers, and takest our often petitions to thee to be an addition to thy glory and thy greatness, as ever upon all occasions, so now, O my God,

---

[12] Mark, xiv. 70.   [13] Ecclus. ii. 18.

I come to thy majesty with two prayers, two supplications. I have meditated upon the jealousy which thou hast of thine own honour, and considered that nothing comes nearer a violating of that honour, nearer to the nature of a scorn to thee, than to sue out thy pardon, and receive the seals of reconciliation to thee, and then return to that sin for which I needed and had thy pardon before. I know that this comes too near to a making thy holy ordinances, thy word, thy sacraments, thy seals, thy grace, instruments of my spiritual fornications. Since therefore thy correction hath brought me to such a participation of thyself (thyself, O my God, cannot be parted), to such an entire possession of thee, as that I durst deliver myself over to thee this minute, if this minute thou wouldst accept my dissolution, preserve me, O my God, the God of constancy and perseverance, in this state, from all relapses into those sins which have induced thy former judgments upon me. But because, by too lamentable experience, I know how slippery my customs of sin have made my ways of sin, I presume to add this petition too, that if my infirmity overtake me, thou forsake me not. Say to my soul, *My son, thou hast sinned, do so no more;*[14] but say also, that though I do, thy spirit of remorse and compunction shall never depart from me. Thy holy apostle, St. Paul, was shipwrecked thrice,[15] and yet still saved. Though the rocks and the sands, the heights and the shallows, the prosperity and the adversity of this world, do diversely threaten me, though mine own leaks endanger me, yet, O God, let me never put myself aboard with Hymenæus, nor *make shipwreck of faith and a good conscience,*[16] and then thy

[14] Ecclus. i. 21.
[15] 2 Cor. xi. 25.   [16] 1 Tim. i. 19.

long-lived, thy everlasting mercy, will visit me,
though that which I most earnestly pray
against, should fall upon me, a relapse
into those sins which I have truly
repented, and thou hast fully
pardoned.

DEATH'S DUEL,

OR, A CONSOLATION TO THE SOUL AGAINST THE DYING LIFE AND LIVING DEATH OF THE BODY.

DELIVERED IN A SERMON AT WHITEHALL, BEFORE
THE KING'S MAJESTY, IN THE BEGINNING
OF LENT, 1630.

BY THAT LATE LEARNED AND REVEREND DIVINE,
JOHN DONNE, DR. IN DIVINITY, AND DEAN
OF ST. PAUL'S, LONDON.

BEING HIS LAST SERMON, AND CALLED BY HIS
MAJESTY'S HOUSEHOLD, THE DOCTOR'S OWN
FUNERAL SERMON.

TO THE READER

THIS sermon was, by sacred authority, styled the author's own funeral sermon, most fitly, whether we respect the time or matter. It was preached not many days before his death, as if, having done this, there remained nothing for him to do but to die; and the matter is of death—the occasion and subject of all funeral sermons. It hath been observed of this reverend man, that his faculty in preaching continually increased, and that, as he exceeded others at first, so at last he exceeded himself. This is his last sermon; I will not say it is therefore his best, because all his were excellent. Yet thus much: a dying man's words, if they concern ourselves, do usually make the deepest impres-sion, as being spoken most feelingly, and with least affectation Now, whom doth it concern to learn both the danger and benefit of death? Death is every man's enemy, and intends hurt to all, though to many he be occasion of greatest good. This enemy we must all combat dying, whom he living did almost conquer, having discovered the utmost of his power, the utmost of his cruelty. May we make such use of this and other the like preparatives, that neither death, when-soever it shall come, may seem terrible, nor life tedious, how long soever it shall last.

DEATH'S DUEL

PSALM LXVIII. 20, *in fine*.

And unto God the Lord belong the issues of death (i.e. from death).

BUILDINGS stand by the benefit of their foundations that sustain and support them, and of their buttresses that comprehend and embrace them, and of their contignations that knit and unite them. The foundations suffer them not to sink, the buttresses suffer them not to swerve, and the contignation and knitting suffers them not to cleave. The body of our building is in the former part of this verse. It is this: *He that is our God is the God of salvation; ad salutes,* of salvations in the plural, so it is in the original; the God that gives us spiritual and temporal salvation too. But of this building, the foundation, the buttresses, the contignations, are in this part of the verse which constitutes our text, and in the three divers acceptations of the words amongst our expositors: *Unto God the Lord belong the issues from death,* for, first, the foundation of this building (that our God is the God of all salvation) is laid in this, that *unto* this *God the Lord belong the issues of death;* that is, it is in his power to give us an issue and deliverance, even then when we are brought to the jaws and teeth of death, and to the lips of that whirlpool, the grave. And so in this acceptation, this *exitus mortis,* this issue of death is *liberatio à morte,* a deliverance from death, and this is the most obvious and most ordinary acceptation of these words, and that upon which our translation lays hold, the *issues from death.* And then, secondly, the buttresses that comprehend and settle this building, that he that is our God is the God of all salvation, are thus raised; *unto God the Lord belong the issues of death,* that is, the disposition and manner of our death; what kind of issue and transmigration we shall have out of this world, whether prepared or sudden, whether violent or natural, whether in our perfect senses or shaken and disordered by sickness, there is no condemnation to be argued out of that, no judgment to be made upon that, for, howsoever they die, *precious in his sight is the death of his saints,* and with him are the issues of death; the ways of our departing out of this life are in his hands. And so in this sense of the words, this *exitus mortis,* the issues of death, is *liberatio in morte,* a deliverance in death; not that God will deliver us from dying, but that he will have a care of us in the hour of death, of what kind soever our passage be. And in this sense and acceptation of the words, the natural frame and contexture doth well and pregnantly administer unto us. And then, lastly, the contignation and knitting of this building, that he that is our God is the God of all salvations, consists in this, *Unto* this *God the Lord belong the issues of death;* that is, that this God the Lord having united and knit both natures in one, and being God, having also come into this world in our flesh, he could have no other means to save us, he could have no other issue out of this world, nor return to his former glory, but by death. And so in this sense, this *exitus mortis*, this issue of death, is *liberatio per mortem*, a deliverance by death, by the death of this God, our Lord Christ Jesus. And this is Saint Augustine's acceptation of the words, and those many and great persons that have adhered to him. In all these three lines, then, we shall look upon these words, first, as the God of power, the Almighty Father rescues his servants from the jaws of death; and then as the God of mercy, the glorious Son rescued us by taking upon himself this issue of death; and then, between these two, as the God of comfort, the Holy Ghost rescues us from all discomfort by his blessed impressions beforehand, that what manner of death soever be ordained for us, yet this *exitus mortis* shall be *introitus in vitam*, our issue in death shall be an entrance into everlasting life. And these three considerations: our deliverance *à morte, in morte, per mortem*, from death, in death, and by death, will abundantly do all the offices of the foundations, of the buttresses, of the contignation, of this our building; that he that is our God is the God of all salvation, because *unto* this *God the Lord belong the issues of death.*

First, then, we consider this *exitus mortis* to be *liberatio à morte*, that with *God the Lord are the issues of death;* and therefore in all our death, and deadly calamities of this life, we may justly hope of a good issue from him. In all our periods and transitions in this life, are so many passages from death to death; our very birth and entrance into this life is *exitus à morte*, an issue from death, for in our mother's womb we are dead, so as that we do not know we live, not so much as we do in our sleep, neither is there any grave so close or so putrid a prison, as the womb would be unto us if we stayed in it beyond our time, or died there before our time. In the grave the worms do not kill us; we breed, and feed, and then kill those worms which we ourselves produced. In the womb the dead child kills the mother that conceived it, and is a murderer, nay, a parricide, even after it is dead. And if we be not dead so in the womb, so as that being dead we kill her that gave us our first life, our life of vegetation, yet we are dead so as David's idols are dead. In the womb we have *eyes and see not, ears and hear not.*[1] There in the womb we are fitted for works of darkness, all the while deprived of light; and there in the womb we are taught cruelty, by being fed with blood, and may be damned, though we be never born. Of our very making in the womb, David says, *I am wonderfully and fearfully made,* and *such knowledge is too excellent for me,*[2] for even that *is the Lord's doing, and it is wonderful in our eyes;*[3] ipse fecit nos, *it is he that made us, and not we ourselves,*[4] nor our parents neither. *Thy hands have made and fashioned me round about,* saith Job, *and* (as the original word is) *thou hast taken pains about me, and yet* (says he) *thou dost destroy me.* Though I be the masterpiece of the greatest master (man is so), yet if thou do no more for me, if thou leave me where thou madest me, destruction will follow. The womb, which should be the house of life, becomes death itself if God leave us there. That which God threatens so often, the shutting of a womb, is not so heavy nor so discomfortable a curse in the first as in the latter shutting, nor in the shutting of barrenness as in the shutting of weakness, when *children are come to the birth, and no strength to bring forth.*[5]

[1] Psalm cxv. 6. [2] Psalm cxxxix. 6. [3] Psalm cxviii. 23.
[4] Psalm c. 3. [5] Isaiah, xxxvii. 3.

It is the exaltation of misery to fall from a near hope of happiness. And in that vehement imprecation, the prophet expresses the highest of God's anger, *Give them, O Lord, what wilt thou give them? give them a miscarrying womb.* Therefore as soon as we are men (that is, inanimated, quickened in the womb), though we cannot ourselves, our parents have to say in our behalf, *Wretched man that he is, who shall deliver him from this body of death?*[6] if there be no deliverer. It must be he that said to Jeremiah, *Before I formed thee I knew thee, and before thou camest out of the womb I sanctified thee.* We are not sure that there was no kind of ship nor boat to fish in, nor to pass by, till God prescribed Noah that absolute form of the ark.[7] That word which the Holy Ghost, by Moses, useth for the ark, is common to all kind of boats, *thebah;* and is the same word that Moses useth for the boat that he was exposed in, that his mother laid him in an ark of bulrushes. But we are sure that Eve had no midwife when she was delivered of Cain, therefore she might well say, *Possedi virum à Domino, I have gotten a man from the Lord,*[8] wholly, entirely from the Lord; it is the Lord that enabled me to conceive, the Lord that infused a quickening soul into that conception, the Lord that brought into the world that which himself had quickened; without all this might Eve say, my body had been but the house of death, and *Domini Domini sunt exitus mortis, To God the Lord belong the issues of death.* But then this *exitus à morte* is but *introitus in mortem;* this issue, this deliverance, from that death, the death of the womb, is an entrance, a delivering over to another death, the manifold deaths of this world; we have a winding-sheet in our mother's womb which grows with us from our conception, and we come into the world wound up in

[6] Rom. vii. 24.   [7] Gen. vi. 14.   [8] Gen. iv. 1.

that winding-sheet, for we come to seek a grave. And as prisoners discharged of actions may lie for fees, so when the womb hath discharged us, yet we are bound to it by cords of hestæ, by such a string as that we cannot go thence, nor stay there; we celebrate our own funerals with cries even at our birth; as though our threescore and ten years' life were spent in our mother's labour, and our circle made up in the first point thereof; we beg our baptism with another sacrament, with tears; and we come into a world that lasts many ages, but we last not. *In domo Patris,* says our Saviour, speaking of heaven, *multæ mansiones,* divers and durable; so that if a man cannot possess a martyr's house (he hath shed no blood for Christ), yet he may have a confessor's, he hath been ready to glorify God in the shedding of his blood. And if a woman cannot possess a virgin's house (she hath embraced the holy state of marriage), yet she may have a matron's house, she hath brought forth and brought up children in the fear of God. *In domo Patris, in my Father's house,* in heaven, there *are many mansions;*[9] but here, upon earth, the *Son of man hath not where to lay his head,*[10] saith he himself. *Nonne terram dedit filiis hominum?* How then hath God given this earth to the sons of men? He hath given them earth for their materials to be made of earth, and he hath given them earth for their grave and sepulchre, to return and resolve to earth, but not for their possession. *Here we have no continuing city,*[11] nay, no cottage that continues, nay, no persons, no bodies, that continue. Whatsoever moved Saint Jerome to call the journeys of the Israelites in the wilderness,[12] mansions; the word (the word is *nasang*) signifies but a journey, but a peregrination. Even the

[9] John xiv. 2. [10] Matt. viii. 20. [11] Heb. xiii. 14.
[12] Exod. xvii. 1.

Israel of God hath no mansions, but journeys, pilgrimages in this life. By what measure did Jacob measure his life to Pharaoh? *The days of the years of my pilgrimage.*[13] And though the apostle would not say *morimur*, that whilst we are in the body we are dead, yet he says, *peri-grinamur*, whilst we are in the body we are but in a pilgrimage, and we are *absent from the Lord*:[14] he might have said dead, for this whole world is but an universal churchyard, but our common grave, and the life and motion that the greatest persons have in it is but as the shaking of buried bodies in their grave, by an earthquake. That which we call life is but *hebdomada mortium*, a week of death, seven days, seven periods of our life spent in dying, a dying seven times over; and there is an end. Our birth dies in infancy, and our infancy dies in youth, and youth and the rest die in age, and age also dies and determines all. Nor do all these, youth out of infancy, or age out of youth, arise so, as the phœnix out of the ashes of another phœnix formerly dead, but as a wasp or a serpent out of a carrion, or as a snake out of dung. Our youth is worse than our infancy, and our age worse than our youth. Our youth is hungry and thirsty after those sins which our infancy knew not; and our age is sorry and angry, that it cannot pursue those sins which our youth did; and besides, all the way, so many deaths, that is, so many deadly calamities accompany every condition and every period of this life, as that death itself would be an ease to them that suffer them. Upon this sense doth Job wish that God had not given him an issue from the first death, from the womb, *Wherefore thou hast brought me forth out of the womb? Oh that I had given up the ghost, and no eye seen me! I should have been as though I had not been.*[15] And not only the impatient

[13] Gen. xlvii. 9.   [14] 2 Cor. v. 6.   [15] Job, x. 18, 19.

Israelites in their murmuring (*would to God we had died by the hand of the Lord in the land of Egypt*),[16] but Elijah himself, when he fled from Jezebel, and went for his life, as that text says, under the juniper tree, requested that he might die, and said, *It is enough now, O Lord, take away my life.*[17] So Jonah justifies his impatience, nay, his anger, towards God himself: *Now, O Lord, take, I beseech thee, my life from me, for it is better to die than to live.*[18] And when God asked him, *Dost thou well to be angry for this?* he replies, *I do well to be angry, even unto death.* How much worse a death than death is this life, which so good men would so often change for death! But if my case be as Saint Paul's case, *quotidiè morior,* that I die daily, that something heavier than death fall upon me every day; if my case be David's case, *tota die mortificamur; all the day long we are killed,* that not only every day, but every hour of the day, something heavier than death fall upon me; though that be true of me, *Conceptus in peccatis, I was shapen in iniquity, and in sin did my mother conceive me* (there I died one death); though that be true of me, *Natus filius iræ,* I was born not only the child of sin, but the child of wrath, of the wrath of God for sin, which is a heavier death: yet *Domini Domini sunt exitus mortis, with God the Lord are the issues of death;* and after a Job, and a Joseph, and a Jeremiah, and a Daniel, I cannot doubt of a deliverance. And if no other deliverance conduce more to his glory and my good, yet he hath the keys of death,[19] and he can let me out at that door, that is, deliver me from the manifold deaths of this world, the *omni die,* and the *tota die,* the every day's death and every hour's death, by that one death, the final dissolution of body and soul, the end of all. But then

16 Exod. xvi. 3.   17 1 Kings, xix. 4.
18 Jonah, iv. 3.   19 Rev. i. 18.

172

is that the end of all? Is that dissolution of body and soul the last death that the body shall suffer (for of spiritual death we speak not now). It is not, though this be *exitus à morte:* it is *introitus in mortem;* though it be an issue from manifold deaths of this world, yet it is an entrance into the death of corruption and putrefaction, and vermiculation, and incineration, and dispersion in and from the grave, in which every dead man dies over again. It was a prerogative peculiar to Christ, not to die this death, not to see corruption. What gave him this privilege? Not Joseph's great proportion of gums and spices, that might have preserved his body from corruption and incineration longer than he needed it, longer than three days, but it would not have done it for ever. What preserved him then? Did his exemption and freedom from original sin preserve him from this corruption and incineration? It is true that original sin hath induced this corruption and incineration upon us; if we had not sinned in Adam, *mortality had not put on immortality*[20] (as the apostle speaks), nor *corruption had not put on incorruption*, but we had had our transmigration from this to the other world without any mortality, any corruption at all. But yet since Christ took sin upon him, so far as made him mortal, he had it so far too as might have made him see this corruption and incineration, though he had no original sin in himself; what preserved him then? Did the hypostatical union of both natures, God and man, preserve him from this corruption and incineration? It is true that this was a most powerful embalming, to be embalmed with the Divine Nature itself, to be embalmed with eternity, was able to preserve him from corruption and incineration for ever. And he was embalmed so, embalmed with the Divine

[20] 1 Cor. xv. 33.

Nature itself, even in his body as well as in his soul; for the Godhead, the Divine Nature, did not depart, but remained still united to his dead body in the grave; but yet for all this powerful embalming, his hypostatical union of both natures, we see Christ did die; and for all his union which made him God and man, he became no man (for the union of the body and soul makes the man, and he whose soul and body are separated by death as long as that state lasts, is properly no man). And therefore as in him the dissolution of body and soul was no dissolution of the hypostatical union, so there is nothing that constrains us to say, that though the flesh of Christ had seen corruption and incineration in the grave, this had not been any dissolution of the hypostatical union, for the Divine nature, the Godhead, might have remained with all the elements and principles of Christ's body, as well as it did with the two constitutive parts of his person, his body and his soul. This incorruption then was not in Joseph's gums and spices, nor was it in Christ's innocency, and exemption from original sin, nor was it (that is, it is not necessary to say it was) in the hypostatical union. But this incorruptibleness of his flesh is most conveniently placed in that; *Non dabis, thou wilt not suffer thy Holy One to see corruption;* we look no further for causes or reasons in the mysteries of religion, but to the will and pleasure of God; Christ himself limited his inquisition in that *ita est, even so, Father, for so it seemeth good in thy sight.* Christ's body did not see corruption, therefore, because God had decreed it should not. The humble soul (and only the humble soul is the religious soul) rests himself upon God's purposes and the decrees of God which he hath declared and manifested, not such as are conceived and imagined in ourselves, though upon some probability, some verisimilitude; so in our present case

174

Peter proceeds in his sermon at Jerusalem, and so Paul in his at Antioch.[21]   They preached Christ to have been risen without seeing corruption, not only because God had decreed it, but because he had manifested that decree in his prophet, therefore doth Saint Paul cite by special number the second Psalm for that decree, and therefore both Saint Peter and Saint Paul cite for it that place in the sixteenth Psalm;[22] for when God declares his decree and purpose in the express words of his prophet, or when he declares it in the real execution of the decree, then he makes it ours, then he manifests it to us.   And therefore, as the mysteries of our religion are not the objects of our reason, but by faith we rest on God's decree and purpose —(it is so, O God, because it is thy will it should be so)— so God's decrees are ever to be considered in the manifestation thereof.   All manifestation is either in the word of God, or in the execution of the decree; and when these two concur and meet it is the strongest demonstration that can be: when therefore I find those marks of adoption and spiritual filiation which are delivered in the word of God to be upon me; when I find that real execution of his good purpose upon me, as that actually I do live under the obedience and under the conditions which are evidences of adoption and spiritual filiation; then, so long as I see these marks and live so, I may safely comfort myself in a holy certitude and a modest infallibility of my adoption.   Christ determines himself in that, the purpose of God was manifest to him; Saint Peter and Saint Paul determine themselves in those two ways of knowing the purpose of God, the word of God before the execution of the decree in the fulness of time.   It was prophesied before, said they, and it is performed now, Christ is risen without seeing corruption.   Now,

[21] Acts, ii. 31; xiii. 35.   [22] Ver. 10.

this which is so singularly peculiar to him, that his flesh should not see corruption, at his second coming, his coming to judgment, shall extend to all that are then alive; their hestæ shall not see corruption, because, as the apostle says, and says as a secret, as a mystery, *Behold I shew you a mystery, we shall not all sleep* (that is, not continue in the state of the dead in the grave), *but we shall all be changed in an instant*, we shall have a dissolution, and in the same instant a redintegration, a recompacting of body and soul, and that shall be truly a death and truly a resurrection, but no sleeping in corruption; but for us that die now and sleep in the state of the dead, we must all pass this posthume death, this death after death, nay, this death after burial, this dissolution after dissolution, this death of corruption and putrefaction, of vermiculation and incineration, of dissolution and dispersion in and from the grave, when these bodies that have been the children of royal parents, and the parents of royal children, must say with Job, *Corruption, thou art my father, and to the worm, Thou art my mother and my sister.* Miserable riddle, when the same worm must be my mother, and my sister and myself! Miserable incest, when I must be married to my mother and my sister, and be both father and mother to my own mother and sister, beget and bear that worm which is all that miserable penury; when my mouth shall be filled with dust, and the *worm shall feed, and feed sweetly*[23] upon me; when the ambitious man shall have no satisfaction, if the poorest alive tread upon him, nor the poorest receive any contentment in being made equal to princes, for they shall be equal but in dust. *One dieth at his full strength, being wholly at ease and in quiet; and another dies in the bitterness of his soul, and never eats with pleasure; but they lie down alike in the dust, and the*

---

[23] Job, xxiv. 20.

worm covers them.[24]   In Job and in Isaiah,[25] it covers
them and is spread under them, *the worm is spread under
thee, and the worm covers thee.*   There are the mats and
the carpets that lie under, and there are the state and the
canopy that hang over the greatest of the sons of men.
Even those bodies that were *the temples of the Holy Ghost*
come to this dilapidation, to ruin, to rubbish, to dust; even
the Israel of the Lord, and Jacob himself, hath no other
specification, no other denomination, but that *vermis
Jacob,* thou worm of Jacob.   Truly the consideration
of this posthume death, this death after burial, that after
God (with whom are the issues of death) hath delivered
me from the death of the womb, by bringing me into the
world, and from the manifold deaths of the world, by
laying me in the grave, I must die again in an incineration
of this flesh, and in a dispersion of that dust.   That that
monarch, who spread over many nations alive, must in
his dust lie in a corner of that sheet of lead, and there but
so long as that lead will last; and that private and retired
man, that thought himself his own for ever, and never
came forth, must in his dust of the grave be published,
and (such are the revolutions of the grave) be mingled
with the dust of every highway and of every dunghill,
and swallowed in every puddle and pond.   This is the
most inglorious and contemptible vilification, the most
deadly and peremptory nullification of man, that we can
consider.   God seems to have carried the declaration of
his power to a great height, when he sets the prophet
Ezekiel in the valley of dry bones, and says, *Son of man,
can these bones live?* as though it had been impossible, and
yet they did; the Lord laid *sinews upon them, and flesh,
and breathed into them, and they did live.*   But in that case
there were bones to be seen, something visible, of which it

[24] Job, xxi. 23, 25, 26.   [25] Isaiah, xiv. 11.

might be said, Can this thing live? But in this death of incineration and dispersion of dust, we see nothing that we call that man's. If we say, Can this dust live? Perchance it cannot; it may be the mere dust of the earth, which never did live, never shall. It may be the dust of that man's worm, which did live, but shall no more. It may be the dust of another man, that concerns not him of whom it was asked. This death of incineration and dispersion is, to natural reason, the most irrecoverable death of all; and yet *Domini Domini sunt exitus mortis, unto God the Lord belong the issues of death;* and by recompacting this dust into the same body, and remaining the same body with the same soul, he shall in a blessed and glorious resurrection give me such an issue from this death as shall never pass into any other death, but establish me into a life that shall last as long as the Lord of Life himself.

And so have you that that belongs to the first acceptation of these words (*unto God the Lord belong the issues of death*); That though from the womb to the grave, and in the grave itself, we pass from death to death, yet, as Daniel speaks, *the Lord our God is able to deliver us, and he will deliver us.*

And so we pass unto our second accommodation of these words (*unto God the Lord belong the issues of death*); that it belongs to God, and not to man, to pass a judgment upon us at our death, or to conclude a dereliction on God's part upon the manner thereof.

Those indications which the physicians receive, and those presagitions which they give for death or recovery in the patient, they receive and they give out of the grounds and the rules of their art; but we have no such rule or art to give a presagition of spiritual death and damnation upon any such indication as we see in any dying man; we see often enough to be sorry, but not to despair; we may be deceived both ways: we use to comfort ourself in the death of a friend, if it be testified that he went away like a lamb, that is, without any reluctation; but God knows that may be accompanied with a dangerous damp and stupefaction, and insensibility of his present state. Our blessed Saviour suffered colluctations with death, and a *sadness even in his soul to death,* and an agony even to a bloody sweat in his body, and expostulations with God, and exclamations upon the cross. He was a devout man who said upon his death-bed, or death-turf (for he was a hermit), *Septuaginta annos Domino servivisti, et mori times?* Hast thou served a good master three-score and ten years, and now art thou loth to go into his presence? Yet Hilarion was loth. Barlaam was a devout man (a hermit too) that said that day he died, *Cogita te hodie cœpisse servire Domino, et hodie finiturum,* Consider this to be the first day's service that ever thou didst thy Master, to glorify him in a Christianly and a constant death, and if thy first day be thy last day too, how soon dost thou come to receive thy wages! Yet Barlaam could have been content to have stayed longer forth. Make no ill conclusions upon any man's lothness to die, for the mercies of God work momentarily in minutes, and many times insensibly to bystanders, or any other than the party departing. And then upon violent deaths inflicted as upon malefactors, Christ himself hath forbidden us by his own death to make any ill conclusion; for his own death had those impressions in it; he was reputed, he was executed as a malefactor, and no doubt many of them who concurred to his death did believe him to be so. Of sudden death there are scarce examples be found in the Scriptures upon good men, for death in battle cannot be called sudden death; but God governs not by examples but by rules, and therefore make no ill conclusion upon sudden death nor upon distempers neither, though perchance accompanied with some words of diffidence and distrust in the mercies of God. The tree lies as it falls, it is true, but it is not the last stroke that fells the tree, nor the last word nor gasp that qualifies the soul. Still pray we for a peaceable life against violent death, and for time of repentance against sudden death, and for sober and modest assurance against distempered and diffident death, but never make ill conclusions upon persons overtaken with such deaths; *Domini Domini sunt exitus mortis, to God the Lord belong the issues of death.* And he received Samson, who went out of this world in such a manner (consider it actively, consider it passively in his own death, and in those whom he slew with himself) as was subject to interpretation hard enough. Yet the Holy Ghost hath moved Saint Paul to celebrate Samson in his great catalogue,[26] and so doth all the church. Our critical day is not the very day of our death, but the whole course of our life. I thank him that prays for me when the bell tolls, but I thank him much more that catechises. me, or preaches to me, or instructs me how to live. *Fac hoc et vive,* there is my security, the mouth of the Lord hath said it, *do this and thou shalt live.* But though I do it, yet I shall die too, die a bodily, a natural death. But God never mentions, never seems to consider that death, the bodily, the natural death. God doth not say, Live well, and thou shalt die well, that is, an easy, a quiet death; but, Live well here, and thou shalt live well for ever. As the first part of a sentence pieces well with the last, and never respects, never hearkens after the parenthesis that comes between, so doth a good life here flow into an eternal life, without any consideration what

[26] Heb. xi.

manner of death we die. But whether the gate of my prison be opened with an oiled key (by a gentle and preparing sickness), or the gate be hewn down by a violent death, or the gate be burnt down by a raging and frantic fever, a gate into heaven I shall have, for from the Lord is the cause of my life, and *with God the Lord are the issues of death.* And further we carry not this second acceptation of the words, as this *issue of death* is *liberatio in morte,* God's care that the soul be safe, what agonies soever the body suffers in the hour of death.

But pass to our third part and last part: As this issue of death is *liberatio per mortem,* a deliverance by the death of another. *Sufferentiam Job audiisti, et vidisti finem Domini,* says Saint James (v. 11), *You have heard of the patience of Job,* says he: all this while you have done that, for in every man, calamitous, miserable man, a Job speaks. Now, *see the end of the Lord,* sayeth that apostle, which is not that end that the Lord proposed to himself (salvation to us), nor the end which he proposes to us (conformity to him), but *see the end of the Lord,* says he, the end that the Lord himself came to, death, and a painful and a shameful death. But why did he die? and why die so? *Quia Domini Domini sunt exitus mortis* (as Saint Augustine, interpreting this text, answers that question),[27] because to this *God our Lord belonged the issues of death. Quid apertius diceretur?* says he there, what can be more obvious, more manifest than this sense of these words? In the former part of this verse it is said, He that is *our God is the God of salvation; Deus salvos faciendi,* so he reads it, the God that must save us. Who can that be, says he, but Jesus? For therefore that name was given him because he was to save us. And to this Jesus, says he, this Saviour,[28] *belong the issues of death;*

---

[27] De Civitate Dei, lib. xvii.   [28] Matt. i. 21.

Nec oportuit eum de hac vita alios exitus habere quam mortis: being come into this life in our mortal nature, he could not go out of this life any other way but by death. *Ideo dictum,* says he, therefore it is said, *to God the Lord belonged the issues of death; ut ostenderetur moriendo nos salvos facturum,* to show that his way to save us was to die. And from this text doth Saint Isidore prove that Christ was truly man (which as many sects of heretics denied, as that he was truly God), because to him, though he were *Dominus Dominus* (as the text doubles it), God the Lord, yet to *him, to God the Lord belonged the issues of death; oportuit eum pati;* more cannot be said than Christ himself says of himself; *These things Christ ought to suffer*,[29] he had no other way but death: so then this part of our sermon must needs be a passion sermon, since all his life was a continual passion, all our Lent may well be a continual Good Friday. Christ's painful life took off none of the pains of his death, he felt not the less then for having felt so much before. Nor will any thing that shall be said before lessen, but rather enlarge the devotion, to that which shall be said of his passion at the time of due solemnization thereof. Christ bled not a drop the less at the last for having bled at his circumcision before, nor will you a tear the less then if you shed some now. And therefore be now content to consider with me how *to this God the Lord belonged the issues of death.* That God, this Lord, the Lord of life, could die, is a strange contemplation; that the Red Sea could be dry, that the sun could stand still, that an oven could be seven times heat and not burn, that lions could be hungry and not bite, is strange, miraculously strange, but supermiraculous that God *could* die; but that God *would* die is an exaltation of that. But even of that also it is a super-

[29] Luke, xxiv. 26.

exaltation, that God should die, must die, and *non exitus* (said Saint Augustine), God the Lord had no issue but by death, and *oportuit pati* (says Christ himself), all this Christ ought to suffer, was bound to suffer; *Deus ultimo Deus*, says David, God is the God of revenges, he would not pass over the son of man unrevenged, unpunished. But then *Deus ultionum libere egit* (says that place), the God of revenges works freely, he punishes, he spares whom he will. And would he not spare himself? he would not: *Dilectio fortis ut mors, love is strong as death*;[30] stronger, it drew in death, that naturally is not welcome. *Si possibile*, says Christ, *if it be possible, let this cup pass*, when his love, expressed in a former decree with his Father, had made it impossible. *Many waters quench not love.*[31] Christ tried many: he was baptised out of his love, and his love determined not there; he mingled blood with water in his agony, and that determined not his love; he wept pure blood, all his blood at all his eyes, at all his pores, in his flagellation and thorns (*to the Lord our God belonged the issues of blood*), and these expressed, but these did not quench his love. He would not spare, nay, he could not spare himself. There was nothing more free, more voluntary, more spontaneous than the death of Christ. It is true, *libere egit*, he died voluntarily; but yet when we consider the contract that had passed between his Father and him, there was an *oportuit*, a kind of necessity upon him: all this *Christ ought to suffer*. And when shall we date this obligation, this *oportuit*, this necessity? When shall we say that began? Certainly this decree by which Christ was to suffer all this was an eternal decree, and was there any thing before that that was eternal? Infinite love, eternal love; be pleased to follow this home, and to consider it seriously, that what

[30] Cant. viii. 6.   [31] *Ibid.* 7.

liberty soever we can conceive in Christ to die or not to die; this necessity of dying, this decree is as eternal as that liberty; and yet how small a matter made he of this necessity and this dying? His Father calls it but a bruise, and but a bruising of his heel[33] (the serpent shall bruise his heel), and yet that was, that the serpent should practise and compass his death. Himself calls it but a baptism, as though he were to be the better for it. I *have a baptism to be baptized with,*[34] and he was in pain till it was accomplished, and yet this baptism was his death. The Holy Ghost calls it joy (*for the joy which was set before him he endured the cross*),[35] which was not a joy of his reward after his passion, but a joy that filled him even in the midst of his torments, and arose from him; when Christ calls his *calicem* a cup, and no worse (*Can ye drink of my cup*)[36], he speaks not odiously, not with detestation of it. Indeed it was a cup, *salus mundo,* a health to all the world. And *quid retribuam,* says David, *What shall I render to the Lord?*[37] Answer you with David, *Accipiam calicem, I will take the cup of salvation;* take it, that cup is salvation, his passion, if not into your present imitation, yet into your present contemplation. And behold how that Lord that was God, yet could die, would die, must die for our salvation. That Moses and Elias talked with Christ in the transfiguration, both Saint Matthew and Saint Mark[38] tells us, but what they talked of, only Saint Luke; *Dicebant excessum ejus,* says he, *They talked of his disease, of his death, which was to be accomplished at Jerusalem.*[39] The word is of his *exodus,* the very word of our text, *exitus,* his *issue by death.* Moses, who in his exodus had pre-

---

[33] Gen. iii. 15.   [34] Luke, xii. 50.   [35] Heb. xii. 2.
[36] Matt. xx. 22.   [37] Psalm cxvi. 12.
[38] Matt. xvii. 3; Mark, ix. 4.   [39] Luke, ix. 31.

figured this issue of our Lord, and in passing Israel out of Egypt through the Red Sea, had foretold in that actual prophecy, Christ passing of mankind through the sea of his blood; and Elias, whose exodus and issue of this world was a figure of Christ's ascension; had no doubt a great satisfaction in talking with our blessed Lord, *de excessu ejus*, of the full consummation of all this in his death, which was to be accomplished at Jerusalem.   Our meditation of his death should be more visceral, and affect us more, because it is of a thing already done.   The ancient Romans had a certain tenderness and detestation of the name of death; they could not name death, no, not in their wills; there they could not say, *Si mori contigerit*, but *si quid humanitas contingat*, not if or when I die, but when the course of nature is accomplished upon me.   To us that speak daily of the death of Christ (he was crucified, dead, and buried), can the memory or the mention of our own death be irksome or bitter? There are in these latter times amongst us that name death freely enough, and the death of God, but in blasphemous oaths and execrations.   Miserable men, who shall therefore be said never to have named Jesus, because they have named him too often; and therefore hear Jesus say, *Nescivi vos*, *I never knew you*, because they made themselves too familiar with him.   Moses and Elias talked with Christ of his death only in a holy and joyful sense, of the benefit which they and all the world were to receive by that.   Discourses of religion should not be out of curiosity, but to edification.   And then they talked with Christ of his death at that time when he was in the greatest height of glory, that ever he admitted in this world, that is, his transfiguration.   And we are afraid to speak to the great men of this world of their death, but nourish in them a vain imagination of immortality and immutability. But *bonum est nobis esse hic* (as Saint Peter said there), *It is good to dwell here*, in this consideraton of his death, and therefore transfer we our tabernacle (our devotions) through some of those steps which God the Lord made to his *issue of death* that day. Take in the whole day from the hour that Christ received the passover upon Thursday unto the hour in which he died the next day. Make this present day that day in thy devotion, and consider what he did, and remember what you have done. Before he instituted and celebrated the sacrament (which was after the eating of the passover), he proceeded to that act of humility, to wash his disciples' feet, even Peter's, who for a while resisted him. In thy preparation to the holy and blessed sacrament, hast thou with a sincere humility sought a reconciliation with all the world, even with those that have been averse from it, and refused that reconciliation from thee? If so, and not else, thou hast spent that first part of his last day in a conformity with him. After the sacrament he spent the time till night in prayer, in preaching, in psalms: hast thou considered that a worthy receiving of the sacrament consists in a continuation of holiness after, as well as in a preparation before? If so, thou hast therein also conformed thyself to him; so Christ spent his time till night. At night he went into the garden to pray, and he prayed prolixious, he spent much time in prayer, how much? Because it is literally expressed, that he prayed there three several times,[40] and that returning to his disciples after his first prayer, and finding them asleep, said, *Could ye not watch with me one hour*,[41] it is collected that he spent three hours in prayer. I dare scarce ask thee whither thou wentest, or how thou disposedst of thyself, when it grew dark and after last

[40] Luke, xxii. 41.   [41] Matt. xxvi. 40.

186

night. If that time were spent in a holy recommendation of thyself to God, and a submission of thy will to his, it was spent in a conformity to him. In that time, and in those prayers, was his agony and bloody sweat. I will hope that thou didst pray; but not every ordinary and customary prayer, but prayer actually accompanied with shedding of tears and dispositively in a readiness to shed blood for his glory in necessary cases, puts thee into a conformity with him. About midnight he was taken and bound with a kiss, art thou not too conformable to him in that? Is not that too literally, too exactly thy case, at midnight to have been taken and bound with a kiss? From thence he was carried back to Jerusalem, first to Annas, then to Caiaphas, and (as late as it was) then he was examined and buffeted, and delivered over to the custody of those officers from whom he received all those irrisions, and violences, the covering of his face, the spitting upon his face, the blasphemies of words, and the smartness of blows, which that gospel mentions: in which compass fell that gallicinium, that crowing of the cock which called up Peter to his repentance. How thou passedst all that time thou knowest. If thou didst any thing that needest Peter's tears, and hast not shed them, let me be thy cock, do it now. Now, thy Master (in the unworthiest of his servants) looks back upon thee, do it now. Betimes, in the morning, so soon as it was day, the Jews held a council in the high priest's hall, and agreed upon their evidence against him, and then carried him to Pilate, who was to be his judge; didst thou accuse thyself when thou wakedst this morning, and wast thou content even with false accusations, that is, rather to suspect actions to have been sin, which were not, than to smother and justify such as were truly sins? Then thou spentest that hour in conformity to him; Pilate found no evidence against him, and therefore to ease himself, and to pass a compliment upon Herod, tetrarch of Galilee, who was at that time at Jerusalem (because Christ, being a Galilean, was of Herod's jurisdiction), Pilate sent him to Herod, and rather as a madman than a malefactor; Herod remanded him (with scorn) to Pilate, to proceed against him; and this was about eight of the clock. Hast thou been content to come to this inquisition, this examination, this agitation, this cribration, this pursuit of thy conscience; to sift it, to follow it from the sins of thy youth to thy present sins, from the sins of thy bed to the sins of thy board, and from the substance to the circumstance of thy sins? That is time spent like thy Saviour's. Pilate would have saved Christ, by using the privilege of the day in his behalf, because that day one prisoner was to be delivered, but they choose Barabbas; he would have saved him from death, by satisfying their fury with inflicting other torments upon him, scourging and crowning with thorns, and loading him with many scornful and ignominious contumelies; but they regarded him not, they pressed a crucifying. Hast thou gone about to redeem thy sin, by fasting, by alms, by disciplines and mortifications, in way of satisfaction to the justice of God? That will not serve, that is not the right way; we press an utter crucifying of that sin that governs thee: and that conforms thee to Christ. Towards noon Pilate gave judgment, and they made such haste to execution as that by noon he was upon the cross. There now hangs that sacred body upon the cross, rebaptized in his own tears, and sweat, and embalmed in his own blood alive. There are those bowels of compassion which are so conspicuous, so manifested, as that you may see them through his wounds. There those glorious eyes grew faint in their sight, so as the sun, ashamed to survive them, departed with his light too. And then that Son of God, who was never from us, and yet had now come a new way unto us in assuming our nature, delivers that soul (which was never out of his Father's hands) by a *new way*, a voluntary emission of it into his Father's hands; for though *to this God our Lord belonged these issues of death*, so that considered in his own contract, he must necessarily die, yet at no breach or battery which they had made upon his sacred body issued his soul; but *emisit*, he gave up the ghost; and as God breathed a soul into the first Adam, so this second Adam breathed his soul into God, into the hands of God.

There we leave you in that blessed dependency, to hang upon him that hangs upon the cross, there bathe in his tears, there suck at his wounds, and lie down in peace in his grave, till he vouchsafe you a resurrection, and an ascension into that kingdom which He hath prepared for you with the inestimable price of his incorruptible blood.   Amen.

Selected Ann Arbor Paperbacks
Works of enduring merit

For a complete list of Ann Arbor Paperback titles write:
THE UNIVERSITY OF MICHIGAN PRESS ANN ARBOR